The London Coffee Guide.

D0785581

Edited by

Jeffrey Young

Author: Allegra Strategies
Reviewers: Richard Ehrlich & Guy Simpson
Researcher: Becky Hindley
Data collection: Beth Hathaway
Photography: Cephas Azariah, Kate Beard, James Bryant, Dan Carter & provided by venues
Design: John Osborne
Cover illustration: John Osborne, inspired by a photograph by Jael Marschner
Website: Tim Spring
Publisher: Allegra Publications Ltd

Allegra
PUBLICATIONS

Published by *Allegra* PUBLICATIONS Ltd © 2017

Walkden House, 10 Melton Street, London, NW1 2EB

Happy Birthday Catarina!
I tried to put some thought
into this present, same way
as you always do :) I really
hope I manage to give you something
that you like! It's been a pleasure
sitting next to you these past
few months. I hope I have learnt
something from the wise person
you are :> I am sure you had
an amazing celebration already
and let today be part of it!
                    Amelie   xxx

Foreword

by **Andrew Tolley**, Co-Founder, Taylor St Baristas

London's dynamic coffee scene had a big year in 2016. The Square Mile is now rife with competition. The Department of Coffee is considering imposing tighter extractions to manage the influx of Caravans. Two characters of yonder years, Harris + Hoole, succumbed to the Black Coffee, but still there is life. The Taylor St Roastery has risen from the ashes. Assuming the hole in the Ozone layer stays closed, another great year in London coffee is ahead, is underway, or Has Bean depending on when you are reading this. One thing is certain, a healthful Dose of Kaffeine will be on hand to keep us going.

London's coffee community has become a role model to the coffee world over the last 9 years. Yet quality coffee is on a relatively new journey. It feels like not so long ago that we would spend countless hours searching out the godshot, exploring brew variables, throwing everything we knew into every shot made in the vain hope of converting another commodity coffee drinker from the dark side. Those were the days. They were the days when craft, raw passion, obsessive quality focus and a united coffee community kept us all going. Sometimes it seems like all those years ago, things were different. But were they really?

The core values that originally drove many of us still prevail. Our coffee quality has never been higher. Our skills continue improving and being enhanced with technology. We are beginning to understand the value of creating and delivering an outstanding customer experience. We know that quality coffee is merely an ingredient in a great café. What matters most is ensuring that we provide the best service possible.

2017 is going to be a challenging year for this great coffee city. Expenses are higher with Brexit's impact on the GBP. There have been asphyxiating council rates rises and increasing costs of labour. General uncertainty combined with higher costs of living, are resulting in declining consumer spending. This is all happening in an ever more competitive retail market. Will 2017 offer any relief from any angle? Nostalgia for the good old days won't help us now: this is uncharted territory. We need to be looking further afield for opportunities, whilst working with each other. The united coffee community of old was one of our greatest assets. Customers, baristas, roasters, and café owners made London's coffee community what it is today.

Can we all survive the challenges of 2017? The Prufrock will be in the pudding. Quality, passion, and craft will continue to improve the overall experience if improving the customer experience is our aim. Our past can still guide the future, so in this spirit, let's offer a very warm welcome to those who are having a first crack at the wonderful world of London coffee featured in this guide.

Contents

Introduction

Welcome to The London Coffee Guide 2017 – the definitive guide to London's independent coffee venues.

Year after year, we endeavour to bring you the crème de la crème of London's leading independent coffee shops, cafés and roasteries. We're here to spill the (coffee) beans on the latest and greatest places to get that all-important caffeinated kick. Whether you're searching for a morning flat white, a lunchtime long black, or an afternoon espresso, we've got plenty of top notch recommendations to get you through the day.

With 30 new venues added to this 2017 edition, we now have a total of 245 profiles in the guide. Due to popular demand, we have now included the icon 'Pet Friendly' for the animal owners and lovers among us. We have also highlighted 'New and Noteworthy'

profiles for you to explore and enjoy. These profiles feature those that we believe to be exciting new additions to the market and will no doubt leave you spoilt for choice.

Our newest article, 'Coffee Cocktails' by Grind, provides insight into this combination of coffee and alcohol. We would like to thank all the industry experts that have contributed to this book, their knowledge and insight inspires a more profound appreciation for the passion, art and experimentation involved in a great cup of coffee.

Allegra is an established leader in consumer and business intelligence for the coffee industry in the UK and Europe. We have drawn on this research as well as experts in the field to compile this edition. We hope you enjoy it.

Photo: Brother Marcus

About the Guide

Ratings

Every venue featured in The London Coffee Guide 2017 has been visited and rated by our expert team. The ratings fall into two distinct categories: Coffee Rating and Overall Rating on a score of 1-5, with 5 being the highest possible score. Customer feedback received via The London Coffee Guide website and app also informs the venue shortlist and the final scores.

Coffee Rating

The Coffee Rating is about much more than just taste in the cup. An excellent coffee experience depends on a host of factors including: barista skills, coffee supplier, equipment, consistency, working processes and coffee presentation. The venue's coffee philosophy and commitment to excellence are also taken into consideration.

Overall Rating

In combination with the Coffee Rating, the Overall Rating reflects the total coffee shop experience for the customer. Factors taken into account include: service, café ambience, venue scale and impact, design and food quality. Feedback from the industry is also taken into consideration.

Key to symbols

Roaster

WiFi available

Alternative brew methods available

Licensed

Coffee beans sold on site

Coffee courses available

Gluten-free products available

Outdoor seating

Venue has a loyalty card

Brunch available at weekends

Milk alternatives available

Cold Brew available

Toilets

Pet friendly

Parent & baby friendly

Participating in UK Coffee Week™

Disabled access

Venues marked as are new to this edition of the Guide.

Venues marked as **NEW & NOTEWORTHY** are recently opened venues we feel are worthy of special mention.

A Brief History of London Coffee Shops

THE EARLY YEARS

800 AD The coffee plant (Coffea) attracts human interest and consumption as early as 800 AD in the Kaffe region of Ethiopia. According to legend, it was an Ethiopian goat herder named Kaldi who first discovered how animated his herd of goats became after chewing on the red berries.

MID 17TH CENTURY

Travellers to Middle Eastern areas such as the Ottoman Empire bring coffee to Europe and Britain.

1650 The first English coffee house is established in Oxford by a Jewish gentleman named Jacob at the Angel in the parish of St Peter.

Coffee houses become meeting places for political and literary debates between artists, intellectuals, merchants and bankers. Such venues are known as Penny Universities, in reference to the one penny entrance fee. They are closely associated with reading and provide pamphlets and newspapers, as well as copious amounts of coffee.

1652 London's first coffee house is established by Pasqua Rosée in St Michael's Alley, Cornhill, London EC3.

1668 Edward Lloyd's Coffee House in Lombard Street becomes a key meeting place for ship owners and marine insurance brokers. Situated on the site occupied by Lloyds bank today, this coffee house likely contributed to London becoming a global hub for insurance and financial services.

1674 The Women's Petition Against Coffee is set up in London in response to men spending less time at home due to the "excessive use of the drying and enfeebling liquor".

1675 There are now more than 3,000 coffee houses across England. King Charles II attempts to outlaw coffee houses as hotbeds of revolution, but following large public protests, his proclamation is revoked after 11 days.

1680 Jonathan's Coffee House is established by Jonathan Miles in Change Alley. It is a place where stockbrokers frequently meet and eventually becomes today's London Stock Exchange.

1706 Thomas Twining opens the first known tea room in London, which can still be found at 216 Strand.

18TH CENTURY

Coffee houses gradually decline in popularity and become more elite establishments, when they start charging more than one penny for entrance. Travelling taverns replace coffee houses as popular social spaces. Coffee also becomes a less important commodity as the East India Company and British trade in general focuses more on tea imports from India.

LAST CENTURY

1894 Lyons opens a chain of tea rooms followed by Lyons Corner Houses in London's West End in 1906.

1923 The Kenya Coffee Company Limited (Kenco) is established and soon begins selling coffee on Vere Street, Mayfair.

1950s Italian-run espresso houses featuring Formica-topped tables are a popular feature of this era, particularly in London's Soho.

1952 Moka Bar opens on Frith Street and is London's first espresso bar.

1971 Starbucks opens its first store at Pike Place Market in Seattle, USA.

First Costa Coffee shop opened by brothers Sergio and Bruno Costa at 9 Newport Street, London.

1978 An early pioneer of artisanal coffee, Monmouth Coffee Company opens in Monmouth Street, Covent Garden.

1986 Pret A Manger is established by college friends Julian Metcalf and Sinclair Beecham.

1992 Fairtrade Foundation is established in London by the Catholic Overseas Development Agency, Christian Aid, Oxfam, Traidcraft, the World Development Movement, and the National Federation of Women's Institutes.

1995 Whitbread Group acquires Costa Coffee with 41 stores and a roastery in Lambeth.

1997 Nescafé opens first Café Nescafé trial stores in London and UK, but closes all outlets several years later.

Gerry Ford acquires five Caffè Nero stores and begins building a chain, which grows to become the third-largest coffee shop brand in the UK.

1998 Starbucks launches in the UK, acquiring 65 Seattle Coffee Company stores for an estimated £52 million.

1999 Allegra Strategies releases the groundbreaking Project Café Report, which predicts a significant boom in coffee shops.

LAST DECADE

2000 Internet cafés grow in popularity during the dotcom era.

Marks & Spencer launches Café Revive concept.

2001 The caffè latte is added to the Consumer Price Index (CPI), the basket of goods the government uses to measure products purchased by a typical British household.

2005 Flat White coffee shop opens in Berwick Street, Soho, setting the stage for further Antipodean influences on coffee in the UK.

2006 The number of branded chain coffee shop outlets exceeds 1,000 in London alone.

2007 James Hoffmann is crowned World Barista Champion and founds Square Mile Coffee Roasters.

2008 The first-ever European Coffee Symposium is held at London's Park Lane Hotel.

2009 A host of new artisanal "third wave" coffee shops open in London.

The UK's Gwilym Davies is crowned World Barista Champion.

2010 Costa, Starbucks and several other mainstream coffee chains launch their versions of the flat white.

The World Barista Championships are held in London at Caffè Culture.

The first edition of The London Coffee Guide is published.

2011 Growth of artisanal coffee shops and micro coffee roasteries in London continues to accelerate with the arrival of Workshop (formerly St. Ali), and Prufrock Coffee.

First-ever London Coffee Festival held at the Old Truman Brewery on Brick Lane.

2012 Roastery/cafés increase in popularity with the opening of Caravan King's Cross, Ozone and TAP Wardour Street.

London Coffee Festival hosts UK Barista Championship finals.

Harris + Hoole opens first London store.

2013 Bulldog Edition opens at Ace Hotel London, in collaboration with Square Mile Coffee Roasters.

2014 Growth of speciality micro-chains, with leading independents such as Grind & Co and Workshop Coffee Co. opening multiple new sites.

2015 Coffee Masters launched at The London Coffee Festival.

Maxwell Colonna-Dashwood wins the UK Barista Championship for the third time.

Risk Capital invests in Small Batch Coffee.

Key openings; Allpress (Dalston), Kaffeine (Eastcastle Street), Origin Coffee (Charlotte Road).

2016 The London Coffee Festival is attended by over 30,000 visitors.

Key openings: Caravan Bankside, Clerkenwell Grind and Workshop Roastery (Vyner Street).

London's West End is synonymous with the city's legendary theatre and music scene, as well as its restaurants, shopping and nightlife. Business people and actors rub shoulders with tourists and urbanites, and the area's café culture is just as diverse.

West End

* NEW
◊ TOP 30

26 Grains

1 Neal's Yard, WC2H 9DP

This tiny, attractive place goes very big on grain-based cooking (hence the name), which is also the subject of a best-selling cookbook published by its owner. Scandinavian in look and feel as well as cooking, it's a place where they want you to enjoy yourself rather than crack the MacBook and work (there's no WiFi). If you're in for a light bite and a drink, there are sandwiches on rye bread, a few sides, sweet stuff, and coffee served in beautiful cups. Milky drinks are the attraction here, with Climpson beans passing through a lovingly attended La Marzocco Linea.

www.26grains.com
⊖ Leicester Square

MON–FRI.	8:00am – 9:30pm
SAT.	9:00am – 9:30pm
SUN.	10:00am – 4:00pm

First opened 2015
Roaster Climpson & Sons
Machine La Marzocco Linea PB, 2 groups
Grinder Nuova Simonelli Mythos One

Espresso	£2.40
Cappuccino	£2.80
Latte	£2.80
Flat white	£2.80

MAP REF. ❶

COFFEE 4.00 / 5

OVERALL 4.00 / 5 ★★★★☆

The Attendant Fitzrovia

27a Foley Street, W1W 6DY

The Attendant is a coffee bar sited in a former Victorian public lavatory, and the astonishing conversion has artfully preserved several original features. Suffice to say that the cups and saucers are not the only porcelain the visitor will encounter. House-roasted coffee is accompanied by a mouth-watering array of sandwiches, cakes, and bakes from artisan producers. Don't be shy to spend a penny or two at one of London's most original coffee venues.

+44(0)20 7637 3794
www.the-attendant.com
⊖ Goodge Street / Oxford Circus

Sister locations Shoreditch

MON-FRI.	8:00am - 6:00pm
SAT.	9:00am - 6:00pm
SUN.	10:00am - 6:00pm

First opened 2013
Roaster The Attendant
Machine La Marzocco Linea PB, 2 groups
Grinder Mazzer Robur E

Espresso	£2.00
Cappuccino	£2.80
Latte	£2.80
Flat white	£2.80

MAP REF. **2**

COFFEE 4.25 / 5   OVERALL 4.25 / 5

5

The Borough Barista Marble Arch

60 Seymour Street, W1H 7JN

Borough Barista is an artisanal alternative to the high street chains that predominate in this part of West London. The venue provides a calm oasis of blonde wood and friendly service just around the corner from Marble Arch. The large downstairs seating area provides ample space for a business meeting, or to spread out with the Saturday papers.

+44(0)20 7563 7222
www.theboroughbarista.com
⊖ Marble Arch

Sister locations St James

MON-FRI.	7:30am – 5:30pm
SAT.	9:00am – 4:00pm
SUN.	Closed

First opened 2011
Roaster The Borough Barista
Machine La Marzocco Linea, 2 groups
Grinder Mazzer Super Jolly, Eureka

Espresso	£2.20
Cappuccino	£3.20
Latte	£3.20
Flat white	£3.20

MAP REF. 3

COFFEE 4.25 / 5	🌰🌰🌰🌰◗	OVERALL 4.25 / 5	★★★★⯪

The Borough Barista St James

15 Charles II Street, SW1Y 4QU

Borough Barista's St James's branch, one of the few coffee joints in this blue-chip area, is surprisingly spacious: a fairly small ground-floor café and a bigger room downstairs. Around half their custom is takeaway for local office workers (no weekend opening). It's an attractive, low-priced lunch spot, and the company's own espresso blend makes a bright cup when pulled through the three-group Linea. Its central location makes Borough a welcome haven for coffee and a sandwich or cake after touring the nearby sights in Piccadilly or Trafalgar Square.

+44(0)20 3272 0222
www.theboroughbarista.com
⊖ Piccadilly Circus

MON-FRI.	7:45am – 5:30pm
SAT-SUN.	Closed

First opened 2013
Roaster The Borough Barista
Machine La Marzocco Linea, 3 groups
Grinder Mazzer Kony x2

Espresso	£2.20
Cappuccino	£3.20
Latte	£3.20
Flat white	£3.20

Sister locations Marble Arch

MAP REF. 4

COFFEE 4.25 / 5	🌰🌰🌰🌰◗	OVERALL 4.00 / 5	★★★★☆

Coffee Island

5 Upper St Martin's Lane, WC2H 9NY

NEW

Two things make Coffee Island such a welcome addition to the Leicester Square scene. One is the outstanding coffee, a wide range roasted by the company itself and featuring a number of lots from 'micro-farms' which they nurture through direct trade. The other is the food, which makes a real effort to excel in quality, freshness, and price. Latte art is great, but let yourself be tempted by the range of filters. Coffee Island is of Greek origin, with this being their first London store. We wouldn't be surprised if more branches follow.

+44(0)20 7836 3007
coffeeisland.co.uk
⊖ Leicester Square

MON-FRI.	7:30am - 9:00pm
SAT-SUN.	9:00am - 9:00pm

First opened 2016
Roaster Coffee Island
Machine Victoria Arduino Black Eagle
Grinder Mahlkönig EK 43, Mahlkönig K30

Espresso	£1.90
Cappuccino	£2.60
Latte	£2.70
Flat white	£2.70

MAP REF. **5**

COFFEE 4.50 / 5		OVERALL 4.25 / 5	

Covent Garden Grind

42 Maiden Lane, WC2E 7LJ

This is a medium-size Grind, with a main dining area on the ground floor and a smaller, slightly quieter (important point here) basement room. Service is a pleasure, delivered efficiently and with a smile. The crowd is a mix of ages and types, with some lone workers, some holding meetings, and some just having a good time with well-made sandwiches and high-quality baked goods. Grind is a fantastic addition to the Covent Garden scene.

grind.co.uk
⊖ Covent Garden

Sister locations Clerkenwell / Holborn / London Bridge / Royal Exchange / Shoreditch / Soho / Exmouth Market / Whitechapel

MON-FRI. 8:00am - 7:00pm
SAT-SUN. 10:00am - 7:00pm

First opened 2016
Roaster The Grind House Espresso
Machine La Marzocco Linea PB, 3 groups x2
Grinder Nuova Simonelli Mythos One x3, Mahlkönig Tanzania

Espresso	£2.20
Cappuccino	£2.90
Latte	£2.90
Flat white	£2.80

MAP REF. **6**

COFFEE
4.25 / 5

OVERALL
4.25 / 5
★ ★ ★ ★ ☆

Curators Coffee Gallery

51 Margaret Street, W1W 8SG

The interior of this Fitzrovia venue dares to deviate from the bare brick and distressed furnishings seen in so many London independents. There is dark wood, a pristine white bar, and kettles made from blazing copper. Spectacular signature drinks such as iced Cascara make neat additions to an already appealing coffee selection. The Curators Coffee Gallery, as the name suggests, is a place to settle in and escape with coffee and art. Whether it's artistry in the cup, on the walls, or indeed on the cup itself, this is a unique coffee shop with a vitality which goes way beyond just the coffee.

+44(0)20 7580 2547
www.curatorscoffee.com
⊖ Oxford Circus

Sister locations Curators Coffee Studio

MON-FRI.	7:30am - 6:30pm
SAT-SUN.	9:00am - 6:00pm

First opened 2014
Roaster Local and international roasters
Machine La Marzocco Strada EP, 3 groups
Grinder Nuova Simonelli Mythos One, Mazzer Robur E, Anfim

Espresso	£2.20
Cappuccino	£2.80
Latte	£2.80
Flat white	£2.80

MAP REF. **7**

Daisy Green

20 Seymour Street, W1H 7HX

Daisy's formula works brilliantly at all its venues. It's all about excellent coffee, friendly service, and Australian-style food with equal emphasis on good health (salads etc.) and wicked self-indulgence (lush baked goods). There's something different, however, at the group's original venue in Marylebone: while all the branches are a pleasure to look at, this one is simply amazing. The upstairs corner room is light and airy, with two big windows. Downstairs is another story altogether, with lovely lighting and a 'garden' area that is simply one of London's most beautiful spaces for eating and drinking. It makes you feel as if you're in a private world, one inhabited by fairies.

Good food flows from the kitchen all the time, with some particularly noteworthy salads and grain-based dishes. And even if you are not there to eat, get a slice of the banana bread to go with your latte or flat white. This area of Marylebone is affluent but not well supplied with casual spots for dining or drinking. That makes Daisy Green even more of an attraction.

MAP REF. **8**

COFFEE 4.25 / 5

OVERALL 4.50 / 5 ★★★★⯪

West End

MON-FRI.	7:00am - 6:30pm
SAT.	8:00am - 6:30pm
SUN.	9:00am - 6:30pm

First opened 2012
Roaster The Roasting Party
Machine La Marzocco FB/80, 2 groups
Grinder Mazzer Robur

Espresso	£2.50
Cappuccino	£2.90
Latte	£2.90
Flat white	£2.90

+44(0)20 7723 3301
www.daisygreenfood.com
⊖ Marble Arch

Sister locations Broadgate Circle / Little Venice / Regent's Place / Portman Village / Royal Festival Hall / Sheldon Square

Department of Coffee and Social Affairs

Covent Garden 19 Slingsby Place, St Martin's Courtyard, WC2E 9AB

The polished design of this branch of Department of Coffee and Social Affairs befits its fashionable Covent Garden location. The café's elegant red awning shades and al fresco seating area are surrounded by the charming shops of St. Martin's Courtyard. The coffee is similarly refined, with two single origin coffees for espresso-based drinks and two roasts for filter. A scrumptious array of neatly presented sandwiches lead the lunch menu, the perfect start to a hard-earned afternoon hitting the boutiques.

www.departmentofcoffee.com

⊖ Leicester Square / Covent Garden

Sister locations Spitalfields Market / Leather Lane / Carnaby Street / Piccadilly / Norton Folgate

| MON-FRI. | 8:00am - 6:00pm |
| SAT-SUN. | 10:30am - 7:00pm |

First opened 2015
Roaster Department of Coffee and Social Affairs
Machine La Marzocco Linea PB, 3 groups
Grinder Mazzer Robur E x2, Mazzer Super Jolly, Mahlkönig Tanzania

Espresso	£2.40
Cappuccino	£2.90
Latte	£2.90
Flat white	£3.00

MAP REF. **9**

| COFFEE 4.50 / 5 | | OVERALL 4.50 / 5 | ★★★★✫ |

The Espresso Room Covent Garden

24 New Row, WC2N 4LA

Formally New Row Coffee, this miniature coffee house is staffed by super-friendly coffee obsessives who discuss latte art in their downtime and prepare the best flat white on a street crammed with other outlets. Daily filter options are available at the bar, along with an enticing lemon drizzle cake, gourmet cookies, and a range of pastries and sandwiches. Fresh almond milk is prepared each day, and the pulp is used to make tasty almond biscuits.

+44(0)20 3583 6949
theespressoroom.london
⊖ Leicester Square / Charing Cross

Sister locations Bloomsbury / Holborn

| MON-FRI. | 7:30am - 7:30pm |
| SAT-SUN. | 9:00am - 7:30pm |

First opened 2011
Roaster Caravan Coffee Roasters and guests
Machine La Marzocco Linea, 2 groups
Grinder Mazzer Robur, Mazzer Super Jolly

Espresso	£2.20
Cappuccino	£2.80 / £3.60
Latte	£2.80 / £3.60
Flat white	£2.80 / £3.60

MAP REF. **10**

| COFFEE 4.25 / 5 | | OVERALL 4.50 / 5 | ★★★★✫ |

Farmstand

42 Drury Lane, WC2B 5AJ

Farmstand is primarily a restaurant, featuring healthy salad boxes. The food's all gluten and dairy-free, and 100 per cent organic. On the coffee front they've gone with beans from Workshop, and they've also done something that's unusual and totally great: in addition to well-made espresso-based drinks from their La Marzocco, they sell filter coffee for just £1 a cup. Healthy for your bank balance. They sell dog food, just in case you're thinking of popping in with your pooch. And if you look at the bottom of your receipt, you're guaranteed a chuckle.

+44(0)20 7240 3866
www.farmstand.co.uk
⊖ Covent Garden

MON-FRI.	7:30am - 9:00pm
SAT.	9:00am - 9:00pm
SUN.	Closed

First opened 2016
Roaster Workshop Coffee
Machine La Marzocco Linea, 2 groups
Grinder Nuova Simonelli Mythos One

Espresso	£2.50
Cappuccino	£2.80
Latte	£2.80
Flat white	£2.80

MAP REF. **11**

West End

COFFEE 4.00 / 5		OVERALL 4.25 / 5	★★★★☆

Fernandez & Wells Somerset House

Somerset House, Strand, WC2R 1LA

This prestigious venue occupies three rooms in one of London's most beautiful buildings. Customers are treated to the usual Fernandez & Wells offering of great meats, cheeses and wines. At the beating heart of the operation is a La Marzocco Linea, handled by a skilled team of baristas who also prepare delicate single-estate filter coffees. This is more than a café - it is a fine food and coffee emporium.

+44(0)20 7420 9408
www.fernandezandwells.com
⊖ Temple

Sister locations Denmark Street / Duke Street / Lexington Street / Somerset House / South Kensington

MON-TUE.	8:00am - 10:00pm
WED-FRI.	8:00am - 11:00pm
SAT.	10:00am - 9:00pm
SUN.	10:00am - 6:00pm

First opened 2011
Roaster Has Bean bespoke blend
Machine La Marzocco Linea PB, 3 groups
Grinder Nuova Simonelli Mythos One

Espresso	£2.60
Cappuccino	£2.95
Latte	£2.95
Flat white	£2.95

MAP REF. **12**

COFFEE 4.25 / 5		OVERALL 4.50 / 5	★★★★☆

The Gentlemen Baristas Store Street

The Building Centre, 26 Store Street, WC1E 7BT

The Gentleman Baristas' original venue, in Southwark, deliberately evokes the spirit of Old London. Their newer one couldn't be more contemporary. It set itself a tricky challenge: combining a dining area, coffee bar, and full kitchen in a small space in the crescent-shaped ground floor of The Building Centre.

Their solution is a complete success. Despite the dinky size, they've managed to accommodate the crowds buying coffee to go while providing comfortable seating (and giving the chefs room enough in back). If you're not en route to someplace else, it's worth sitting here. Coffee is mostly from their own roastery, and the espresso blend is outstanding when married to milk.

GB's food deserves serious attention. The menu has been developed by a highly skilled and quality-conscious chef who tries to make as much as possible in-house, including relishes, sauces, butter, and ricotta. It's nothing fancy, sandwiches and a soup of the day, but within those constraints there's a lot of flair and close attention to detail. Even in an area where there's no shortage of competition, Gentleman Baristas is right up there with the very best.

MAP REF.

COFFEE	OVERALL
4.50 / 5	4.50 / 5

MON-FRI.	8:00am – 5:00pm	
SAT-SUN.	Closed	

First opened 2016
Roaster The Gentlemen Baristas,
Neighbourhood Coffee
Machine Faema E71
Grinder Mazzer Major E, Mazzer Kony

Espresso	£2.00
Cappuccino	£2.60
Latte	£2.60
Flat white	£2.60

www.thegentlemenbaristas.com
🚇 Goodge Street

Sister locations Union Street

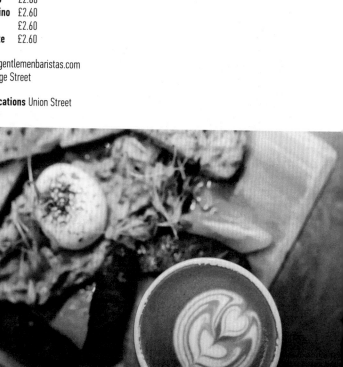

Gitane

60 Great Titchfield Street, W1W 7QF

Gitane serves great coffee, all Ozone beans and all espresso-based. Drink it outside or at the tables in front, with a good view through the big windows. But that's not all that Gitane does. This lovely Fitzrovia spot is a showcase for food heavily influenced by Persian cooking (the owner is originally from Iran). It's a café menu in the day, with more 'serious' fare taking over at night and served at the tables in back. And if all you want is coffee and a pastry, you've come to the right place.

+44(0)20 7631 5269
www.gitanelondon.co.uk
⊖ Oxford Circus

| MON–FRI. | 8:00am – 10:30pm |
| SUN. | Closed |

First opened 2012
Roaster Ozone Coffee Roasters
Machine La Marzocco Linea, 2 groups
Grinder Mazzer Robur E

Espresso	£2.40
Cappuccino	£2.90
Latte	£2.80
Flat white	£2.80

MAP REF. 14

COFFEE
4.25 / 5

OVERALL
4.25 / 5 ★★★★

Kaffeine Eastcastle Street

15 Eastcastle Street, W1T 3AY

West End

This second beautiful Kaffeine has a subtly different feel from the original: it's a tad bigger, and instead of bare brick has a sleek look featuring high ceilings, wood both pale and dark, and a beautiful copper counter. Seating is on high stools or benches. What hasn't changed one bit is the superb quality of the coffee. Skilled baristas pull beautiful Square Mile beans through the Black Eagle espresso machine with assurance and consistency. The changing menu of in house produced soups, salads, sandwiches and baked goods makes for great eating from breakfast through the late afternoon.

+44(0)20 3730 5878
www.kaffeine.co.uk
⊖ Oxford Circus

Sister locations Great Titchfield Street

MON-FRI.	7:30am – 6:00pm
SAT.	8:30am – 6:00pm
SUN.	9:00am – 5:00pm

First opened 2015
Roaster Square Mile Coffee Roasters
Machine Victoria Arduino Black Eagle, 3 groups
Grinder Nuova Simonelli Mythos One Clima Pro

Espresso	£2.10
Cappuccino	£3.00
Latte	£3.00
Flat white	£2.90

MAP REF. **15**

 COFFEE 4.75 / 5    **OVERALL** 4.75 / 5

Kaffeine Great Titchfield Street

66 Great Titchfield Street, W1W 7QJ

Since opening in 2009, Kaffeine has established itself as one of London's pre-eminent coffee venues. Australian owner Peter Dore-Smith sets the bar high and his team strives to provide the best possible experience for all, from casual lunch customers to coffee experts. This café is distinguished by its impeccable attention to detail, from the stylish wooden interior to the food made fresh on site. Kaffeine has developed a loyal following and remains a source of inspiration for London's coffee community. A second Kaffeine is on nearby Eastcastle Street.

+44(0)20 7580 6755
www.kaffeine.co.uk
⊖ Oxford Circus

MON-FRI.	7:30am - 6:00pm
SAT.	8:30am - 6:00pm
SUN.	9:00am - 5:00pm

First opened 2009
Roaster Square Mile Coffee Roasters
Machine Synesso Cyncra, 3 groups
Grinder Mazzer, Mahlkönig EK 43

Espresso	£2.10
Cappuccino	£3.00
Latte	£3.00
Flat white	£2.90

Sister locations Eastcastle Street

MAP REF. **16**

| COFFEE 4.75 / 5 | | OVERALL 5 / 5 |  |

Kin Cafe

22 Foley Street, W1W 6DT

West End

Everything from the food to the furniture furthers Kin's mission to source in an ethical and socially responsible way. Their sourdough bread, for example, is baked by Better Health Bakery, an East London social enterprise employing adults recovering from mental illness. Kin's soothing interior of clean lines and muted tones falls somewhere between a Scandinavian kitchen and Japanese tea room. It's an environment to calm the soul, providing a serene backdrop to the sumptuous menu of superfood salads, quiche, cakes, and baked goodies.

+44(0)20 7998 4720
www.kincafe.co.uk
⊖ Goodge Street / Oxford Circus

MON–FRI.	7:30am – 5:30pm
SAT.	10:00am – 5:00pm
SUN.	Closed

First opened 2014
Roaster Clifton Coffee Roasters
Machine La Marzocco Linea, 2 groups
Grinder Anfim, Mahlkönig EK 43

Espresso	£2.20
Cappuccino	£2.80 / £3.30
Latte	£2.80 / £3.30
Flat white	£2.80

MAP REF. **17**

 COFFEE 4.25 / 5

 OVERALL 4.25 / 5 ★★★★⯪

Lantana Fitzrovia

13 Charlotte Place, W1T 1SN

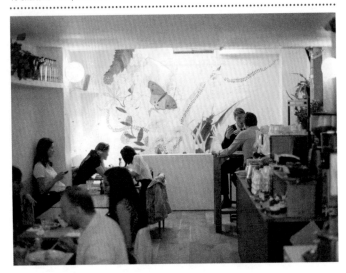

Stylish and understated Fitzrovia favourite Lantana has gone from strength to strength since opening in 2008. This café and eatery is always abuzz with chatter and filled with loyal patrons, particularly during the weekend when its legendary brunch menu has customers queuing out the door. The coffee here is of a consistently high quality, both on the main premises and at the second shopfront next door that caters just for takeaway traffic.

+44(0)20 7637 3347
www.lantanacafe.co.uk
⊖ Goodge Street / Tottenham Court Road

Sister locations Shoreditch / Camden

| MON-FRI. | 8:00am - 6:00pm |
| SAT-SUN. | 9:00am - 5:00pm |

First opened 2008
Roaster Alchemy bespoke blend
Machine La Marzocco FB/80, 3 groups
Grinder Mazzer Robur E, Anfim

Espresso	£2.30
Cappuccino	£2.80
Latte	£2.80
Flat white	£2.80

MAP REF.

   COFFEE 4.50 / 5 OVERALL 4.50 / 5 ★★★★⯪

Monmouth Coffee Company Covent Garden

27 Monmouth Street, WC2H 9EU

West End

This is where the Monmouth phenomenon began, back in 1978. The original Monmouth roastery occupied this site until 2007 when it moved to Bermondsey. The interior here is simple, focusing attention on the coffee. Wooden booths encourage strangers to share conversation and trade ideas, continuing the grand tradition of the capital's first coffee houses. Monmouth Coffee is nothing short of a London institution, and more often than not, queues snake out of the door, but it's definitely worth the wait.

+44(0)20 7232 3010
www.monmouthcoffee.co.uk
⊖ Covent Garden

MON–SAT. 8:00am – 6:30pm
SUN. Closed

First opened 1978
Roaster Monmouth Coffee Company
Machine La Marzocco Linea, 3 groups
Grinder Mazzer Robur E

Espresso	£1.70
Cappuccino	£2.70
Latte	£2.70
Flat white	£2.70

Sister locations Borough / Bermondsey

MAP REF. **19**

COFFEE 4.50 / 5

OVERALL 4.50 / 5 ★★★★⯪

Monocle Café

18 Chiltern Street, W1U 7QA

Monocle Café is an impeccably curated coffee shop belonging to Tyler Brûlé's global current affairs, business and lifestyle magazine empire. The café bears all the hallmarks of Monocle's slick aspirational brand and design-conscious outlook. Every item is meticulously sourced, from the midcentury-style furniture, right down to the teaspoons and barista aprons. A small kitchen downstairs serves up plates of elegant fare, and the Swedish cinnamon buns and Japanese cakes deserve a special mention.

+44(0)20 7135 2040
cafe.monocle.com
⊖ Baker Street

MON-WED.	7:00am - 7:00pm
THU-FRI.	7:00am - 8:00pm
SAT.	8:00am - 8:00pm
SUN.	8:00am - 7:00pm

First opened 2013
Roaster Allpress Espresso
Machine La Marzocco Linea PB, 2 groups
Grinder Mazzer Robur E, Mazzer Super Jolly

Espresso	£2.50
Cappuccino	£3.00
Latte	£3.00
Flat white	£3.00

MAP REF. 20

 22

 COFFEE 4.25 / 5

 OVERALL 4.25 / 5 ★★★★☆

Notes Trafalgar Square

31 St Martin's Lane, WC2N 4ER

Notes Trafalgar Square was the first venue opened by Brazilian coffee entrepreneur Fabio Ferreira. Occupying a stunning room with high ceilings, large mirrors, and a refined yet welcoming atmosphere, this is a coffee house that looks to London's past for its decor but is distinctly forward-looking in its coffee philosophy. The progressive coffee menu is complemented by a range of fine foods. In the evening, the café turns into a wine bar, and theatre-goers in the know drop by to sample the range of excellent wines, spirits, cheeses, and charcuterie.

+44(0)20 7240 0424
www.notes-uk.co.uk
⊖ Charing Cross / Leicester Square

Sister locations Canary Wharf / Gherkin / King's Cross / Moorgate

MON-WED.	7:30am - 9:00pm
THU-FRI.	7:30am - 10:00pm
SAT.	9:00am - 10:00pm
SUN.	10:00am - 6:00pm

First opened 2010
Roaster Notes Coffee Roasters
Machine La Marzocco FB/80, 3 groups
Grinder Nuova Simonelli Mythos

Espresso	£2.20 / £2.40
Cappuccino	£2.70 / £2.90
Latte	£2.70 / £2.90
Flat white	£2.70 / £2.90

MAP REF.

 COFFEE 4.50 / 5   OVERALL 4.50 / 5

23

The Providores and Tapa Room

109 Marylebone High Street, W1U 4RX

Run by New Zealand chef Peter Gordon, The Providores and Tapa Room is a fusion restaurant, café, and wine bar with a distinct South Pacific flavour. The ground floor Tapa room features a huge Rarotongan tapa cloth on one wall and heaves with people at breakfast, while the dining room upstairs caters for a more formal lunch and dinner crowd. Coffee is supplied by Volcano Coffee Works, the perfect accompaniment to a delicious brunch at this highly popular venue.

+44(0)20 7935 6175
www.theprovidores.co.uk
⊖ Baker Street / Bond Street

Sister locations Kopapa

MON-FRI.	8:00am – 10:30pm
SAT.	9:00am – 11:00pm
SUN.	9:00am – 10:30pm

First opened 2001
Roaster Volcano Coffee Works
Machine La Marzocco GB/5, 2 groups
Grinder Mazzer Super Jolly

Espresso	£2.35
Cappuccino	£3.25
Latte	£3.25
Flat white	£3.25

MAP REF. 22

COFFEE 4.25 / 5 🫘🫘🫘🫘◗

OVERALL 4.25 / 5 ★★★★⯪

Sharps Coffee Bar

9 Windmill Street, W1T 2JF

At Sharps, a barber shop and coffee bar complement one another without a whisker of encroachment. Sharps is one of the few coffee shops to offer coffee from celebrated Berlin roastery, The Barn, and also offers guest coffees on every last week of the month. The café feels very neatly pulled together as a whole; every detail from the trim tiling to clean-cut branding befits this dapper Fitzrovia location.

+44(0)20 7636 8688
www.sharpsbarbers.com
⊖ Goodge Street

MON-FRI.	8:00am – 5:00pm
SAT.	10:00am – 5:00pm
SUN.	Closed

First opened 2013
Roaster The Barn and guests
Machine Kees van der Westen Spirit, 3 groups
Grinder Mahlkönig K30, Mahlkönig EK 43

Espresso	£2.00
Cappuccino	£2.40
Latte	£2.60
Flat white	£2.40

MAP REF. 23

COFFEE 4.50 / 5 🫘🫘🫘🫘🫘

OVERALL 4.50 / 5 ★★★★⯪

Store Street Espresso Store Street

40 Store Street, WC1E 7DB

West End

This exciting venue joined the burgeoning foodie scene on Store Street in 2010 and crowds of hungry students and creatives have been flocking here ever since for the great coffee and electric atmosphere. The café itself is stylish and light-filled, with an ambience that encourages customers to linger for leisure, study or work. A passionate team of baristas serve Square Mile coffee on a top-of-the-range Black Eagle coffee machine, and regularly offer guest coffees from up-and-coming roasters.

www.storestespresso.co.uk
🚇 Goodge Street

Sister locations Tavistock Place

MON-FRI.	7:30am - 7:00pm	
SAT.	9:00am - 6:00pm	
SUN.	10:00am - 5:00pm	

First opened 2010
Roaster Square Mile Coffee Roasters and guests
Machine Victoria Arduino Black Eagle, 3 groups
Grinder Nuova Simonelli Mythos x2, Mahlkönig EK 43

Espresso	£2.20 / £2.60
Cappuccino	£2.80
Latte	£2.80
Flat white	£2.80

MAP REF. **24**

COFFEE 4.50 / 5

OVERALL 4.50 / 5 ★★★★⯪

25

TAP Coffee Rathbone Place

26 Rathbone Place, W1T 1JD

TAP Coffee was one of the first London coffee bars to break with convention and offer a selection of different espresso blends. The venue's design theme blends burnished wood and steel with attractive features such as a Belfast sink filled with chilled drinks, and the classic delivery bicycle mounted above the door. The Rathbone Place store is a popular hangout for Fitzrovia admen, who mastermind advertising campaigns over perfectly-poured flat whites.

+44(0)20 7580 2163
www.tapcoffee.co.uk
⊖ Tottenham Court Road / Goodge Street

Sister locations Tottenham Court Road / Wardour Street

MON-FRI.	8:00am – 7:00pm
SAT.	10:00am – 6:00pm
SUN.	Closed

First opened 2010
Roaster TAP Coffee
Machine Nuova Simonelli Aurelia II T3, 3 groups
Grinder Mazzer Robur E, Mazzer Kony E, Mazzer Super Jolly E, Mahlkönig Tanzania

Espresso	£2.20
Cappuccino	£2.80
Latte	£2.80
Flat white	£2.80

MAP REF. **25**

 COFFEE 4.50 / 5

 OVERALL 4.50 / 5 ★★★★⯪

TAP Coffee Tottenham Court Road

114 Tottenham Court Road, W1T 5AH

TAP's unbranded facade sets it apart on chain-dominated Tottenham Court Road. Look closer and you'll notice a vintage bicycle suspended above the doorway, a motif that also graces the takeaway cups and ingeniously illustrated loyalty cards. The interior fuses exposed light bulbs, copper piping, and white ceramic that recalls London's Victorian heyday. The attention to detail displayed towards the design is also evident in the coffee preparation. Baristas use separate blends for espresso and milk coffees, and single origin beans can be sampled on filter.

+44(0)20 7580 2163
www.tapcoffee.co.uk
🚇 Warren Street

Sister locations Rathbone Place
/ Wardour Street

MON-FRI. 7:30am - 7:30pm
SAT-SUN. 10:00am - 6:00pm

First opened 2011
Roaster TAP Coffee
Machine Nuova Simonelli Aurelia Competizione, 3 groups
Grinder Mazzer Robur E, Mazzer Kony E, Mazzer Super Jolly E, Mahlkönig Tanzania

Espresso	£2.20
Cappuccino	£2.80
Latte	£2.80
Flat white	£2.80

MAP REF.

COFFEE 4.75 / 5

OVERALL 4.50 / 5

Taylor St Baristas Mayfair

22 Brooks Mews, W1K 4DY

Hidden away down a little mews, this small café is popular with suited-up professionals. The sunlit interior features dark antique furniture, a slate floor, and reclaimed church pews. The Taylor St independent chain has built its reputation on consistently excellent coffee and, just as importantly, well-trained and friendly staff. This is especially true at the Mayfair store, where baristas and customers banter freely with one another, and has led to the creation of the competitive 'Super frequent coffee freaks' loyalty blackboard.

+44(0)20 7629 3163
www.taylor-st.com
Bond Street

Sister locations Liverpool Street / Shoreditch / Canary Wharf / Monument / Bank / South Quay / St Paul's

MON-FRI.	7:30am - 5:30pm
SAT-SUN.	Closed

First opened 2011
Roaster Taylor St Baristas
Machine La Marzocco Linea, 3 groups
Grinder Mazzer Kony E, Mahlkönig EK 43, Nuova Simonelli Mythos

Espresso	£2.00
Cappuccino	£2.80 / £3.20
Latte	£2.80 / £3.20
Flat white	£2.80 / £3.70

MAP REF. 27

COFFEE 4.75 / 5   OVERALL 4.50 / 5

Timberyard Seven Dials

7 Upper St Martin's Lane, WC2H 9DL

This Seven Dials outpost has the usual Timberyard charm. Split over two floors, the comfortable seating area downstairs is perfect for working away with a laptop, and two dedicated rooms are available to hire for business meetings or other gatherings. Customers can try the excellent coffee brewed by Chemex as well as espresso, and the stellar tea service also deserves a special mention. Each teapot is served with a timer to ensure optimal brew time.

www.tyuk.com
⊖ Leicester Square / Covent Garden

Sister locations Soho

MON-FRI.	8:00am – 7:00pm
SAT.	9:00am – 6:00pm
SUN.	10:00am – 6:00pm

First opened 2014
Roaster Climpson & Sons, The Barn and guests
Machine La Marzocco Linea PB
Grinder Nuova Simonelli Mythos, Mahlkönig EK 43

Espresso	£2.40
Cappuccino	£3.00
Latte	£3.00
Flat white	£2.80

MAP REF. 28

COFFEE 4.50 / 5

OVERALL 4.75 / 5 ★★★★✦

Workshop Coffee Fitzrovia

80a Mortimer Street, W1W 7FE

TOP
35

Workshop Fitzrovia harks back to London's imperial zenith; its intricate tiling and gold details invoke Victorian grandeur. And then there's that bar: a sovereign slab of Madagascan granite, imbued with a magnetism which demands your gaze and touch. The coffee is precisely what you'd expect from Workshop: light-roasted and delicious. The baristas are efficient and deliberate, engaging customers with utmost politeness. There's a sense of mastery about the place; an irrefutable statement that in speciality coffee, London is enjoying a new heyday with Workshop at the vanguard.

www.workshopcoffee.com

⊖ Oxford Circus

Sister locations Marylebone / Clerkenwell / Holborn

MON-FRI.	7:00am - 7:00pm
SAT-SUN.	9:00am - 6:00pm

First opened 2014
Roaster Workshop Coffee
Machine La Marzocco Linea PB, 3 groups
Grinder Nuova Simonelli Mythos One x3

Espresso	£2.60
Cappuccino	£3.10
Latte	£3.30
Flat white	£3.10

MAP REF. **29**

COFFEE
4.75 / 5

OVERALL
4.75 / 5
★★★★⯪

Workshop Coffee Marylebone

1 Barrett Street, W1U 1AX

At this smaller outpost of Workshop, coffee is a science and its baristas are laureates of the highest order. This is coffee at its best, brewed with clinical precision and minute attention to detail. Re-locating here from the former premises on Wigmore Street, Workshop's Marylebone outpost is the blueprint for a new kind of coffee bar. Simple bench seating runs the length of two walls and a small selection of pastries is enshrined behind polished glass. A range of Workshop's own beans and coffee-making equipment is available to purchase.

www.workshopcoffee.com
⊖ Bond Street

Sister locations Clerkenwell / Holborn / Fitzrovia

| **MON-FRI.** | 7:00am - 7:00pm |
| **SAT-SUN.** | 9:00am - 6:00pm |

First opened 2015
Roaster Workshop Coffee
Machine Synesso Hydra, 3 groups
Grinder Mazzer Robur E x2, Mazzer Major E, Mahlkönig Tanzania, Mahlkönig EK 43

Espresso	£2.60
Cappuccino	£3.10
Latte	£3.30
Flat white	£3.10

MAP REF. 30

 COFFEE 4.75 / 5 OVERALL 4.50 / 5  ★★★★✰

Famous for its outrageous nightlife, Soho is also well-known for its cutting-edge bars, clubs and restaurants. This spirit of experimentation and adventure extends to coffee and many of London's most exciting artisanal cafés can be found here.

Soho

Bar Termini

7 Old Compton Street, W1D 5JE

Bar Termini is half coffee bar and half cocktail bar, with the two sides run by figures of distinction: Marco Arrigo of Illy on the coffee side, Tony Conigliaro of 69 Colebrooke Row, Zetter Town House and other top bars on the cocktail side. It offers little in the way of food, so all the focus is on 'the liquids' – and what liquids they are. Intriguingly, they don't believe in delaying delivery of your coffee by doing latte art: if you want to create your own, they'll give you a barista's pitcher.

+44(0)7860 945 018
www.bar-termini.com
Leicester Square

MON-THU.	11:30am – 1:00pm
FRI-SUN.	10:00am – 1:00am

First opened 2015
Roaster Illy
Machine Faema Legend E61, 2 groups
Grinder Faema

Espresso	£1.00 / £2.50
Cappuccino	£3.50
Latte	£3.50
Flat white	£3.50

MAP REF.

COFFEE 4.00 / 5	OVERALL 4.00 / 5 ★★★★☆

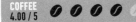

Damson & Co

21 Brewer Street, W1F 0RL

By day, Damson is a café serving first breakfast then lunch from a small kitchen in back. In the evening, it becomes a bar serving an interesting selection of small-distiller gins, and then a restaurant majoring on small plates, salads, intriguing flatbreads and cheese and charcuterie plates. If you're going just for coffee, you're making a smart move. The head barista has a CV that's five-star all the way, and does great things with Ozone beans and the three-group La Marzocco Strada. A real Soho star. Note: while they don't have loyalty cards, they do have a 'neighbourhood discount.'

www.damsonandco.com
⊖ Piccadilly Circus

MON–FRI. 9:00am – 11:00pm
SAT–SUN. 10:00am – 11:00pm

First opened 2013
Roaster Ozone Coffee Roasters
Machine La Marzocco Strada, 3 groups
Grinder La Marzocco Volcano

Espresso	£3.00
Cappuccino	£3.00
Latte	£3.00
Flat white	£3.00

MAP REF. 32

COFFEE 4.25 / 5	OVERALL 4.25 / 5 ★★★★⯪

TOP 35: Department of Coffee and Social Affairs
Carnaby Street 3 Lowndes Court, W1F 7HD

Occupying a light, modern space just off Carnaby Street, this branch of Department (formerly known as Speakeasy) is home to some of London's most talented baristas. The café offers an impressive choice of coffee beans: two espresso roasts complemented by two different single origins on filter. There's more to this stylish coffee bar than meets the eye: Department encourages a hands-on approach to coffee making, operating a coffee school in the dedicated downstairs space.

www.departmentofcoffee.com
⊖ Oxford Circus

Sister locations Spitalfields Market / Norton Folgate / Leather Lane / Piccadilly / Covent Garden

MON–FRI. 8:00am – 7:00pm
SAT. 9:30am – 8:00pm
SUN. 10.00am – 7:00pm

First opened 2011
Roaster Department of Coffee and Social Affairs
Machine La Marzocco FB/80, 3 groups
Grinder Mazzer Robur E x2, Mazzer Super Jolly, Mahlkönig Tanzania

Espresso	£2.40
Cappuccino	£2.90
Latte	£2.90
Flat white	£3.00

MAP REF. 33

COFFEE 4.50 / 5	OVERALL 4.50 / 5 ★★★★⯪

Department of Coffee and Social Affairs
Piccadilly 15 Sherwood Street, W1F 7ED

This compact venue (formerly named Tonic) is a modern and sophisticated take on the traditional Italian espresso bar. Department is ideal for picking up an expertly-made brew before dashing to your next Soho appointment. Owing to the small space, it's not the best place to spread out with the broadsheets. Alongside Department's house-roasted espresso blend, coffee aficionados will delight in the rotating range of single origin filter coffees.

www.departmentofcoffee.com
🚇 Piccadilly Circus

Sister locations Spitalfields Market / Norton Folgate / Leather Lane / Carnaby Street / Covent Garden

MON-FRI.	7:30am – 5:00pm
SAT.	9:30am – 4:30pm
SUN.	Closed

First opened 2013
Roaster Department of Coffee and Social Affairs and guests
Machine La Marzocco FB/80, 2 groups
Grinder Mazzer Robur E x2, Mazzer Super Jolly, Mahlkönig Tanzania

Espresso	£2.40
Cappuccino	£2.90
Latte	£2.90
Flat white	£3.00

MAP REF. **34**

COFFEE
4.25 / 5

OVERALL
4.25 / 5
★★★★⭐

Fernandez & Wells Denmark Street

1-3 Denmark Street, WC2H 8LP

One of the early proponents of speciality coffee in London, Fernandez & Wells is a food and drink emporium satisfying the most fervid foodie. Do you have a hankering for ham? Try the Iberian cured meats from Brindisa. Are you partial to pressed juice? Freshly squeezed blood orange for you. When it comes to coffee, Jorge Fernandez is as experienced as they come, having managed Monmouth's Covent Garden store before most Londoners had sipped their first flat white. The impressive Denmark Street site is a temple to temptation which must be visited.

+44(0)20 3302 9799
www.fernandezandwells.com
⊖ Tottenham Court Road

Sister locations Duke Street / Lexington Street / Somerset House / South Kensington

MON-TUE.	8:00am - 9:00pm
WED-FRI.	8:00am - 11:00pm
SAT.	9:00am - 10:00pm
SUN.	10:00am - 6:00pm

First opened 2014
Roaster Has Bean bespoke blend
Machine La Marzocco Linea PB, 3 groups
Grinder Nuova Simonelli Mythos One

Espresso	£2.60
Cappuccino	£2.95
Latte	£2.95
Flat white	£2.95

MAP REF.

COFFEE 4.25 / 5

OVERALL 4.25 / 5 ★★★★⯪

37

Flat White

17 Berwick Street, W1F 0PT

Established in 2005, Flat White was perhaps the first café to bring Antipodean-style coffee to the UK. For a time it became a London coffee institution, celebrated as a pioneer of third wave coffee in the capital. The venue has changed management several times since those heady days, but fortunately there's a continued focus on quality. The interior has been refreshed and customers can expect a range of beans from Dark Arts, pulled through an impressive 4-group Synesso, affectionately dubbed "The Great White".

+44(0)20 7734 0370
www.flatwhitesoho.co.uk
⊖ Oxford Circus / Tottenham Court Road

Sister locations Milkbar

MON–FRI.	8:00am – 6:00pm
SAT.	9:00am – 6:00pm
SUN.	9:30am – 6:00pm

First opened 2005
Roaster Dark Arts Coffee
Machine Synesso Hydra, 4 groups
Grinder Nuova Simonelli Mythos, Mazzer

Espresso	£2.40
Cappuccino	£3.00
Latte	£3.00
Flat white	£2.80

MAP REF. **36**

COFFEE 4.50 / 5	OVERALL 4.50 / 5
🫘🫘🫘🫘🫘	★★★★½

Milkbar

3 Bateman Street, W1D 4AG

Milkbar emerged from beneath the wing of legendary Flat White to become one of Soho's most popular café venues. It has grown into a mecca for Kiwis and Aussies longing for a taste of home, and a place of discovery for Londoners experiencing the third wave's daringly light roasts. After a period of transition, this much-loved Antipodean café is returning to form. The baristas' disarming informality, together with the venue's youthful, grungy feel make it a popular hangout for Soho creatives.

+44(0)20 7287 4796
⊖ Tottenham Court Road / Leicester Square

Sister locations Flat White

MON-FRI.	8:00am - 5:30pm
SAT-SUN.	9:30am - 6:00pm

First opened 2008
Roaster Dark Arts Coffee
Machine La Marzocco FB/80, 3 groups
Grinder Ditting, Nuova Simonelli x2

Espresso	£2.40
Cappuccino	£3.00
Latte	£3.00
Flat white	£2.80

MAP REF.

Rapha Cycle Club Soho

85 Brewer Street, W1F 9ZN

The perfectionism Rapha applies to its cycling gear is readily apparent in its approach to coffee; the espresso here is extraordinarily good. Try a shot made with Alchemy beans, pulled through a La Marzocco FB/80. Bike locks are available for those arriving on two wheels, and the vintage Italian cycling memorabilia adds to the café's sense of energy and momentum. Coffee is no afterthought here; Rapha has established itself as a coffee destination in its own right.

+44(0)20 7494 9831
www.rapha.cc
🚇 Piccadilly Circus

Sister locations Spitalfields

MON–FRI.	8:00am – 7:00pm
SAT.	8:30am – 6:30pm
SUN.	11:00am – 5:00pm

First opened 2012
Roaster Allpress Espresso, The Barn, Notes Coffee Roasters
Machine La Marzocco FB/80
Grinder Mazzer Super Jolly x 2, Anfim, Mahlkönig Tanzania

Espresso	£2.30
Cappuccino	£3.00
Latte	£3.20
Flat white	£3.00

MAP REF. **38**

COFFEE
4.50 / 5

OVERALL
4.50 / 5
★ ★ ★ ★ ⯪

Sacred Ganton Street

13 Ganton Street, W1F 9BL

The Sacred empire extends across four London locations but this is where it all began back in 2005. Owner Tubbs Wanigasekera is a proud New Zealander and this shines through in the decor and relaxed atmosphere that characterises this busy café. While the main upstairs area has a pleasing openness that extends out into the bustle of Carnaby Street, couches in the mellow basement area offer a cosy refuge in which to sip a cup of the delicious new 'Auckland' espresso blend.

www.sacredcafe.com
⊖ Oxford Circus

Sister locations The Strand / Highbury Studios / Westfield

MON–WED. 7:30am – 10:00pm
THU–SAT. 7:30am – 12:00am
SUN. 10:00am – 9:00pm

First opened 2005
Roaster Sacred Gourmet Blend, Sacred Auckland Blend
Machine La Marzocco Linea, 3 groups
Grinder Anfim Super Caimano, Mazzer Super Jolly

Espresso	£2.10
Cappuccino	£2.90 / £3.10
Latte	£2.90 / £3.10
Flat white	£2.90 / £3.10

MAP REF. **39**

COFFEE
4.25 / 5

OVERALL
4.50 / 5

Soho Grind

19 Beak Street, W1F 9RP

The Grind & Co. empire is on a mission to make coffee sexy, and what better neighbourhood to do it in than Soho? The second store from entrepreneur David Abrahamovitch and Australian DJ Kaz James is an enticing coffee and cocktail den complete with sanguine lighting and bass soundtrack. Satisfy your coffee cravings with a seductive flat white, then descend the steps - beneath the neon sign promising 'French lessons given downstairs' - to the basement speakeasy for an espresso martini.

+44(0)20 7287 7073
www.sohogrind.com
⊖ Piccadilly Circus

Sister locations Clerkenwell / Covent Garden / Holborn / London Grind / Royal Exchange / Shoreditch

MON-THU.	7:30am - 11:00pm
FRI.	7:30am - 12:00am
SAT.	9:00am - 12:00am
SUN.	9:00am - 7:00pm

First opened 2014
Roaster The Grind House Espresso
Machine La Marzocco Linea PB, 3 groups
Grinder Nuova Simonelli Mythos One x2, Mahlkönig Tanzania

Espresso	£2.20
Cappuccino	£2.90 / £3.20
Latte	£2.90 / £3.20
Flat white	£2.80

MAP REF. **40**

COFFEE
4.50 / 5

OVERALL
4.50 / 5 ★★★★⯪

TAP Coffee Wardour Street

193 Wardour Street, W1F 8ZF

TAP Coffee's Soho venue is an impressive statement in coffee bar design. Two rows of tables draw the eye towards the magnificent Probat roaster. Low-hung spotlights highlight the interior's bare wood and gleaming steel fixtures. TAP serves its excellent house-roasted 'Jack of Spades' blend, and single origins at the dedicated brew bar. Connoisseurs will also appreciate the green tea offered as a palate cleanser. Visitors can expect exceptionally high standards from one of London's most accomplished coffee destinations.

+44(0)20 7580 2163
www.tapcoffee.co.uk
⊖ Tottenham Court Road

Sister locations Rathbone Place / Tottenham Court Road

MON-FRI.	8:00am - 7:00pm
SAT.	10:00am - 6:00pm
SUN.	12:00pm - 6:00pm

First opened 2012
Roaster TAP Coffee
Machine Nuova Simonelli Aurelia T3, 3 groups
Grinder Mazzer Robur E, Mazzer Kony E, Mazzer Super Jolly E, Mahlkönig Tanzania

Espresso	£2.20
Cappuccino	£2.80
Latte	£2.80
Flat white	£2.80

MAP REF. 41

COFFEE 4.75 / 5　🫘🫘🫘🫘🫘

OVERALL 4.50 / 5　★★★★⯨

43

Timberyard Soho

4 Noel Street, W1F 8GB

This second branch of Timberyard is their biggest, and one of the two floors is a members-only work space. Most customers are plugged into their devices, but it's a good place to talk and the noise level is reasonable even when it's rammed. As at the other branch, ordering an espresso means being offered a choice of two styles, one each from their two main roasters. Both are very well made. The food menu emphasises 'wellness', but there's still conceptual space for an array of enticing sweet stuff. Oreo™ Brownie, anyone?

www.tyuk.com

⊖ Oxford Circus / Tottenham Court Road

Sister locations Seven Dials

MON-FRI.	8:00am - 7:00pm
SAT-SUN.	11:00am - 6:00pm

First opened 2015
Roaster Climpson & Sons, The Barn and guests
Machine Nuova Simonelli Aurelia T3
Grinder Mahlkönig EK 43, Nuova Simonelli Mythos One

Espresso	£2.40
Cappuccino	£3.00
Latte	£3.00
Flat white	£2.80

MAP REF. 42

COFFEE 4.50 / 5

OVERALL 4.50 / 5 ★★★★½

Dotted with beautiful squares and grand architecture, Bloomsbury offers refined, contemplative surroundings to enjoy coffee. Home to thinkers for centuries, the neighbourhood is anchored by numerous academic institutions and the imposing British Museum, as well as boasting a wealth of literary connections. Busy Holborn to the south is frequented by lawyers and journalists, conducting business in and around the many cafés.

Holborn & Bloomsbury

The Black Penny

34 Great Queen Street, WC2B 5AA

This popular Covent Garden café uses their own The Roastery Department blend. There is evident skill behind the machine, so we're not in doubt of continuing fine coffee making. Where quality shines also brightly is in the food, which rises several notches above the West End café norm. Delicious baked goods, sandwiches and salads are all outstanding. You can get a takeaway, but the back room is a splendidly comfortable place to spend part of your morning, lunchtime or even a full leisurely afternoon.

+44(0)20 7242 2580
www.theblackpenny.co.uk
⊖ Covent Garden / Holborn

MON-FRI.	8:00am – 6:00pm
SAT.	9:00am – 6:00pm
SUN.	9:00am – 5:00pm

First opened 2015
Roaster The Roastery Department
Machine La Marzocco PB, 3 groups
Grinder Mahlkönig Twin, Mahlkönig EK 43

Espresso	£2.30
Cappuccino	£2.80
Latte	£2.80
Flat white	£2.80

MAP REF. **43**

 COFFEE
4.25 / 5

OVERALL
4.50 / 5

The Espresso Room Bloomsbury

31-35 Great Ormond Street, WC1N 3HZ

Despite The Espresso Room's pocket-sized proportions, the amiable baristas manage the queue with practiced ease, pulling shots on the Synesso Hydra with utmost precision. This tiny espresso bar is widely considered one of London's very best, with a focus on coffee quality few others can match. Join the line of hospital staff, lawyers, and dapper Lamb's Conduit fashionistas to discover why.

+44(0)7760 714 883
www.theespressoroom.com
⊖ Russell Square

Sister locations Covent Garden / Holborn

MON-FRI.	7:30am - 5:00pm
SAT.	9:00am - 3:30pm
SUN.	Closed

First opened 2009
Roaster Caravan Coffee Roasters and guests
Machine Synesso Hydra, 2 groups
Grinder Mazzer Robur E, Mahlkönig EK 43

Espresso	£1.80 / £2.20
Cappuccino	£2.80 / £3.40
Latte	£2.80 / £3.40
Flat white	£2.80 / £3.40

MAP REF. **44**

COFFEE 4.75 / 5	🫘🫘🫘🫘🫘	OVERALL 4.25 / 5	★★★★⯪

The Espresso Room Holborn

23 Southampton Row, WC1B 5HA

Raising the banner for craft coffee in Holborn, formally FreeState, The Espresso Room's experienced baristas serve excellent coffee with a dose of American-style enthusiasm. Beautifully mismatched furniture and an old school gym bench add character to the sunny interior. Customers with time to linger can opt for single estate filter coffee served at the dedicated brew bar.

+44(0)20 7998 1017
www.freestatecoffee.co.uk
⊖ Holborn

Sister locations Bloomsbury / Covent Garden

MON-FRI.	7:00am - 7:00pm
SAT-SUN.	8:30am - 6:00pm

First opened 2013
Roaster Caravan Coffee Roasters
Machine La Marzocco Strada EP, 3 groups
Grinder Mazzer Robur E x2, Mahlkönig EK 43

Espresso	£2.20
Cappuccino	£2.80 / £3.50
Latte	£2.80 / £3.50
Flat white	£2.80 / £3.30

MAP REF. **45**

COFFEE 4.50 / 5	🫘🫘🫘🫘🫘	OVERALL 4.25 / 5	★★★★⯪

Half Cup

100-102 Judd St, WC1H 9NT

You know how you sometimes walk into an unfamiliar coffee place and think, 'I wish I lived around the corner'? Half Cup is that sort of place. It looks great, you get a great big smile and hello when you set foot inside the door, and Nude beans from the Linea turn into excellent coffee whether milky or black. Your fellow customers might be device-bound workers, office-lunchers, or discerning tourists. At weekends it's a thriving local scene. The food is priced very fairly for this part of town, and the carrot cake has a devoted following.

+44(0)7595 625 703
www.halfcup.co.uk
⊖ King's Cross

MON-FRI.	8:00am - 8:00pm
SAT-SUN.	9:00am - 5:00pm

First opened 2014
Roaster Nude Coffee Roasters
Machine La Marzocco Linea, 2 groups
Grinder Compak K10,
Nuova Simonelli Mythos One

Espresso	£2.20
Cappuccino	£2.70
Latte	£2.70
Flat white	£2.70

MAP REF. 46

50

COFFEE 4.25 / 5

OVERALL 4.25 / 5 ★★★★½

Holborn Grind

199 High Holborn, WC1V 7BD

Grind is very much in the pink, with a rapidly expanding portfolio of stores. Grind use their own house espresso, which is also the base of their famous espresso martinis, not to mention the hot flat white Russian. The bar's huge windows and corner location adjoining the newly-opened Hoxton Hotel affords customers the chance to see and be seen. Holborn Grind is helping to transform this previously transient neighbourhood into a vibrant food and drink destination.

+44(0)20 3693 3400
www.holborngrind.com
⊖ Holborn

Sister locations Clerkenwell / Covent Garden / London Grind / Shoreditch / Soho / Royal Exchange / Exmouth Market / Whitechapel

MON-WED.	7:00am - 10:30pm
THU.	7:00am - 11:00pm
FRI.	7:00am - 12:00am
SAT.	9:00am - 12:00am
SUN.	9:00am - 7:00pm

First opened 2014
Roaster The Grind House Espresso
Machine La Marzocco Linea PB, 3 groups
Grinder Nuova Simonelli Mythos One x3, Mahlkönig Tanzania

Espresso	£2.20
Cappuccino	£2.90 / £3.20
Latte	£2.90 / £3.20
Flat white	£2.80

MAP REF.

COFFEE 4.50 / 5

OVERALL 4.50 / 5 ★★★★⯪

Hopper Coffee

4 Roger Street, WC1N 2JX

Hopper is a tiny place (it was originally a sandwich takeaway) and has just a few seats if you want to eat and drink on the premises. But it's memorable nonetheless, simply because the coffee is exceptionally good and the food exceptionally inexpensive. (Sandwiches here are roughly half the price of some comparable coffee shops.) The beans come from Coffee Compass, and their espresso blend is round and sweet enough to drink without sugar. Locals love the place: at times the queue snakes right around the corner. It's easy to see why.

⊖ Holborn

MON-FRI.	7:00am – 5:00pm
SAT-SUN.	Closed

First opened 2016
Roaster Coffee Compass
Machine La Marzocco Linea AV, 2 groups
Grinder Mazzer Major

Espresso	£1.70
Cappuccino	£2.40
Latte	£2.40
Flat white	£2.40

MAP REF. 48

COFFEE 4.25 / 5

OVERALL 4.25 / 5 ★★★★✫

Hubbard & Bell

199-206 High Holborn, WC1V 7BD

Hubbard & Bell is a café, bar and grill occupying a swathe of the open plan foyer of the Hoxton Hotel. This slick, midcentury-inspired space hums with activity as hotel guests mingle with fashionably dressed media workers. The talented barista team have a background at some of London's top cafés, ensuring that the standard of coffee preparation is consistently high. Hubbard & Bell demonstrates that with the right approach, top-notch coffee can be served in a modern, fast-paced hotel environment.

+44(0)20 7661 3030
www.hubbardandbell.com
⊖ Holborn

Sister locations Barber & Parlour

MON-FRI.	7:00am – 2:00am
SAT.	8:00am – 2:00am
SUN.	8:00am – 12:00pm

First opened 2014
Roaster Origin Coffee Roasters and guests
Machine La Marzocco Strada, 3 groups
Grinder Nuova Simonelli Mythos x2, Mahlkönig EK 43

Espresso	£2.50
Cappuccino	£2.80
Latte	£2.80
Flat white	£2.80

MAP REF. **49**

| COFFEE 4.50 / 5 | | OVERALL 4.50 / 5 | ★★★★✦ |

Knockbox Coffee

29 Lamb's Conduit Street, WC1N 3NG

With its array of outfitters, Lamb's Conduit Street is a destination for the dapper man about town. The road is also home to another well-pulled-together outfit in the shape of Knockbox Coffee. Turkish owner, Mete Dogrul, has a meticulous eye for detail, creating the furniture and fittings himself with plywood and copper. Occupying a sunny corner, the café is perfectly positioned for people-watching. Relax with a Workshop coffee whilst tucking into a hearty sandwich or a glorious pastry.

+44(0)20 3489 7325
www.knockboxcoffee.com
⊖ Russell Square / Holborn

MON-FRI.	7:30am – 6:00pm
SAT.	8:00am – 5:00pm
SUN.	9:00am – 5:00pm

First opened 2014
Roaster Workshop Coffee
Machine Synesso Cyncra, 2 groups
Grinder Mazzer Major

Espresso	£2.50
Cappuccino	£2.90
Latte	£2.90
Flat white	£2.90

MAP REF. **50**

| COFFEE 4.25 / 5 |  | OVERALL 4.25 / 5 | ★★★★✦ |

Workshop Coffee Holborn

60a Holborn Viaduct, EC1A 2FD

Workshop Holborn is a coffee bar for perfectionists. Its design can be summed up in just one word: uncompromising. The interior details look like they were agonised over during many long nights of planning. Even the two La Marzoccos, gleaming on the marble bar, have been stripped of their metal fins for a more streamlined appearance. The meticulously dosed coffee flows from immaculate portafilters into satisfyingly weighty porcelain cups. Workshop's exacting philosophy might not be to everybody's taste, but there's no question it has redefined what we've come to expect from a coffee bar.

www.workshopcoffee.com
🚇 Farringdon / Chancery Lane

MON-FRI.	7:00am - 6:00pm
SAT-SUN.	Closed

First opened 2014
Roaster Workshop Coffee
Machine La Marzocco Linea PB, 3 groups and 2 groups
Grinder Nuova Simonelli Mythos One x3, Mazzer Major, Mahlkönig EK 43 x2

Espresso	£2.60
Cappuccino	£3.10
Latte	£3.30
Flat white	£3.10

Sister locations Marylebone / Fitzrovia / Clerkenwell

MAP REF. **51**

COFFEE 4.75 / 5	OVERALL 4.75 / 5

54

EXCEPTIONAL
COFFEE

www.matthewalgie.com | 0800 263333

Formerly hubs of manufacturing and enterprise, the districts of Farringdon and Clerkenwell now house smart offices, loft apartments, night clubs and restaurants. Some of the most exciting coffee venues in town can also be found here, making this the new heart of London's burgeoning coffee culture.

Farringdon & Clerkenwell

Caravan Exmouth Market

11-13 Exmouth Market, EC1R 4QD

Caravan roastery and restaurant is a popular fixture on the diverse Exmouth Market food and coffee scene. This modern dining venue is always busy, particularly on sunny days when patrons spill out onto the pavement, and plenty of options on the menu make this a popular destination for a weekend brunch or casual dinner.

As well as espresso, a wide variety of coffee brewing methods are on offer, allowing patrons to appreciate the full range of flavours found in Caravan's delicious house roasts.

+44(0)20 7833 8115
www.caravanonexmouth.co.uk
⊖ Angel / Farringdon

Sister locations King's Cross

MON-WED.	8:00am - 11:00pm
THU-FRI.	8:00am - 12:00am
SAT.	10:00am - 12:00am
SUN.	10:00am - 10:30pm

First opened 2010
Roaster Caravan Coffee Roasters
Machine Faema Teorema, 3 groups
Grinder Mazzer Robur E x2, Ditting KR 804, Mahlkönig K30

Espresso	£2.00
Cappuccino	£2.60
Latte	£2.60
Flat white	£2.60

MAP REF. **52**

COFFEE 4.75 / 5

OVERALL 4.50 / 5

59

Clerkenwell Grind

2-4 Old Street, EC1V 9AA

Grind marches on, spreading ceaselessly across the capital with new openings. Well, there are openings and there's Clerkenwell Grind, which is on a new level for this energetic group. This is the biggest and most ambitious Grind yet, a 100-cover restaurant/café/bar that keeps long hours - and very long hours Thursday through Saturday. The menu covers everything from breakfast to dinner, with particularly well-priced starters and mains, and cocktails are a big feature on the drinks list.

Most of the ground-floor space is for dining, with beautiful light fixtures and comfortable long banquettes along the walls, but there's a smaller café at the front if you just want coffee. And if you go outside mealtimes, in the morning or afternoon, you can have the dining room pretty much to yourself for the price of a flat white. The three-group Linea shares the honours with single-origin filter, and the professionalism of Grind's customer service is never less than assured.

This is one of those rare places where you could start out with breakfast, drink coffee all day, and finish with a wee-hours nightcap. A serious addition to the thriving Clerkenwell scene.

MAP REF. **53**

COFFEE 4.50 / 5	OVERALL 4.50 / 5

MON-WED.	7:00am - 11:00pm
THU-FRI.	7:00am - 2:00am
SAT.	8:00am - 2:00am
SUN.	9:00am - 7:00pm

Sister locations Covent Garden / Holborn / London Bridge / Royal Exchange / Shoreditch / Soho / Exmouth Market / Whitechapel

First opened 2016
Roaster The Grind House Espresso
Machine La Marzocco Linea PB, 3 groups
Grinder Nuova Simonelli Mythos One x2, Mahlkönig Tanzania

Espresso	£2.20
Cappuccino	£2.90
Latte	£2.90
Flat white	£2.90

grind.co.uk
⊖ Barbican

Farringdon & Clerkenwell

Department of Coffee and Social Affairs
Leather Lane 14-16 Leather Lane, EC1N 7SU

Department of Coffee and Social Affairs is a key player on the booming Farringdon coffee scene. Occupying a former ironmonger's premises across two shopfronts, this generous space features an unpolished wood and exposed brick theme with plentiful seating. Department roasts its own coffee in collaboration with Ben Presland, an expert coffee roaster known for roasting for the Tate and UK Barista Champion Maxwell Colonna-Dashwood.

+44(0)20 7419 6906
www.departmentofcoffee.co.uk
⊖ Chancery Lane / Farringdon

Sister locations Spitalfields Market / Norton Folgate / Carnaby Street / Piccadilly / Covent Garden

MON–FRI.	7:00am – 5:30pm
SAT.	9:30am – 4:00pm
SUN.	Closed

First opened 2010
Roaster Department of Coffee and Social Affairs
Machine La Marzocco Linea PB3, 3 groups
Grinder Mazzer Robur E x2, Mazzer Super Jolly, Mahlkönig Tanzania

Espresso	£2.40
Cappuccino	£2.90
Latte	£2.90
Flat white	£3.00

MAP REF. **54**

COFFEE 4.50 / 5   **OVERALL** 4.50 / 5 ★★★★⯨

Fix

161 Whitecross Street, EC1Y 8JL

Discreetly occupying a former pub adjacent to the Whitecross St Market, Fix is a spacious and stylish place to drop in for a coffee and bite to eat. Fix serves a Climpson & Sons blend custom-roasted to their exact specification. Big leather couches, well-chosen vintage furniture, and quirky light fittings make this a comfortable and dynamic space in which to hang out. Creatives and visitors to the Whitecross Street market keep Fix buzzing on weekdays.

+44(0)20 7998 3878
www.fix-coffee.co.uk
⊖ Old Street / Barbican

Sister locations Fix 126

MON-FRI.	7:00am – 6:00pm
SAT.	8:00am – 6:00pm
SUN.	9:00am – 6:00pm

First opened 2009
Roaster Climpson & Sons, Caravan Coffee Roasters
Machine La Marzocco Linea, 3 groups
Grinder Nuova Simonelli Mythos x2, Mazzer Robur E

Espresso	£1.60 / £2.00
Cappuccino	£2.50 / £2.70
Latte	£2.50 / £2.70
Flat white	£2.50

MAP REF. **55**

COFFEE
4.25 / 5

OVERALL
4.25 / 5 ★★★★⯪

Granger & Co Clerkenwell

Clerkenwell Green, 50 Sekforde Street, EC1R 0HA

NEW

Bill Granger's dictionary of restaurant design does not contain the word 'unattractive'. Even by his standards, however, Granger Clerkenwell is a stunner. Huge and sprawling over two floors of a window-lined corner spot, it makes an incredibly soothing spot for chilling outside mealtimes. (They welcome third-space cadets when the place isn't busy.) Espresso-based drinks are well made, but the real star here is cold drip, served on ice. Sip it slowly with a piece of cake on the side. If you dawdle long enough, it will be cocktail hour and then dinnertime.

+44(0)20 7251 9032
grangerandco.com
⊖ Farringdon

Sister locations Notting Hill / King's Cross

MON–FRI.	7:00am – 11:00pm
SAT.	9:00am – 11:00pm
SUN.	10:00am – 6:00pm

First opened 2014
Roaster Allpress Espresso
Machine La Marzocco Linea AV, 3 groups
Grinder Mazzer Robur, Mazzer Super Jolly

Espresso	£2.80
Cappuccino	£2.80
Latte	£2.80
Flat white	£2.80

MAP REF. **56**

COFFEE
4.50 / 5

OVERALL
4.50 / 5
★★★★✫

Ground Control

61 Amwell Street, EC1R 1UR

The Ethiopian Coffee Company's mission is to showcase the very best coffees from this unique part of Africa, including Yirgacheffe, Harrar, and Sidamo. The company's Clerkenwell café, Ground Control, combines traditional Ethiopian curios with the sharp, space-age lines of a Kees van der Westen Mirage coffee machine. The company also retails beans at the Real Food Market behind the Southbank Centre (Fridays-Sundays) and Partridges Specialist Food Market in Chelsea (Saturdays).

+44(0)20 7502 1201
www.theethiopiancoffeecompany.co.uk
⊖ Angel

MON.	7:30am - 4:00pm
TUE-FRI.	7:30am - 5:00pm
SAT.	8:00am - 5:00pm
SUN.	9:00am - 4:00pm

First opened 2012
Roaster The Ethiopian Coffee Company
Machine Kees van der Westen Mirage, 2 groups
Grinder Anfim Titanium

Espresso	£2.50
Cappuccino	£2.90
Latte	£2.90
Flat white	£2.80

MAP REF. **57**

COFFEE 4.50 / 5 🫘🫘🫘🫘🫘

OVERALL 4.25 / 5 ★★★★✭

Look Mum No Hands! Clerkenwell

49 Old Street, EC1V 9HX

Look Mum No Hands! is one of the city's best destinations for those who love bikes and coffee in equal measure. This lively café and workshop is decorated with bicycles, bike parts, and vintage cycling memorabilia. A range of British craft beer is available on tap, and during the Tour de France, this place is a full-on party zone. The café frequently hosts a range of bike-related events, including cyclist speed dating nights. If you love bikes, coffee, or both, a No Hands! is an essential pit-stop.

+44(0)20 7253 1025
www.lookmumnohands.com
Old Street / Barbican

MON–FRI.	7:30am – 10:00pm
SAT.	8:30am – 10:00pm
SUN.	9:00am – 10:00pm

First opened 2010
Roaster Square Mile Coffee Roasters and guests
Machine Kees van der Westen Mirage, 3 groups
Grinder Anfim x2, Mythos

Espresso	£2.20
Cappuccino	£2.90
Latte	£2.90
Flat white	£2.70

MAP REF. 58

COFFEE 4.50 / 5

OVERALL 4.50 / 5 ★★★★½

Prufrock Coffee

23-25 Leather Lane, EC1N 7TE

Photo: Nicholas Friesen

Prufrock has achieved legendary status in London, and international recognition for its progressive methods and tireless pursuit of coffee excellence. Founded by Gwilym Davies (2009 World Barista Champion) and Jeremy Challender, Prufrock is a premier destination to see unusual brew methods and sample rare coffees. Prufrock features one of the broadest ranges of 85+ coffees that you'll find in London, featuring guest roasts from The Barn, Five Elephant and Koppi just to name a few, so if you are looking for something new they can certainly help. The space also incorporates an SCAE accredited coffee training school catering to novices and barista champions alike. With a fantastic space and welcoming staff, Prufrock is one of the best.

+44(0)20 7242 0467
www.prufrockcoffee.com
⊖ Farringdon / Chancery Lane

MON-FRI.	7:30am - 6:00pm
SAT-SUN.	10:00am - 5:00pm

First opened 2011
Roaster Square Mile Coffee Roasters and multiple guests
Machine Victoria Arduino Black Eagle Gravimetric, 3 groups
Grinder Mahlkönig EK 43, Mazzer ZM, Nuova Simonelli Mythos One Clima Pro

Espresso	£2.20
Cappuccino	£2.80 / £3.00
Latte	£3.00
Flat white	£2.80

MAP REF. **59**

COFFEE	OVERALL	
5 / 5	4.75 / 5	★★★★★

Workshop Coffee Clerkenwell

27 Clerkenwell Road, EC1M 5RN

TOP 35

Workshop Coffee has experienced a meteoric rise. This temple to speciality coffee contains a café, restaurant, and roastery, spanning multiple floors of an industrial themed space. A remarkable 'living wall' of plants adds a dash of green to the raw brick and steel. Attracting top talent from the UK, Australia, and the US, Workshop is a young company with a reputation for coffee roasting excellence. An array of single origins and Workshop's own popular espresso blend are crafted on-site, and their coffee is now a frequent sight in some of the capital's finest coffee bars.

+44(0)20 7253 5754
www.workshopcoffee.com
⊖ Farringdon

Sister locations Marylebone / Holborn / Fitzrovia

MON.	7:30am - 6:00pm
TUE-FRI.	7:30am - 7:00pm
SAT-SUN.	8:00am - 6:00pm

First opened 2011
Roaster Workshop Coffee
Machine La Marzocco Linea PB, 3 groups, La Marzocco Linea, 2 groups
Grinder Nuova Simonelli Mythos One

Espresso	£2.60
Cappuccino	£3.10
Latte	£3.30
Flat white	£3.10

MAP REF.

    COFFEE 5 / 5 OVERALL 5 / 5  ★★★★★

EXCEPTIONAL COFFEE

www.matthewalgie.com | 0800 263333

MATTHEW ALGIE

London's centre of finance and commerce may not boast the sheer number of cafés as Soho or the West End, but several recent high-profile openings have rapidly transformed its coffee fortunes. The City is surprisingly quiet at weekends (and many coffee bars open Monday to Friday only), so the area is best experienced during the bustling work week.

The City

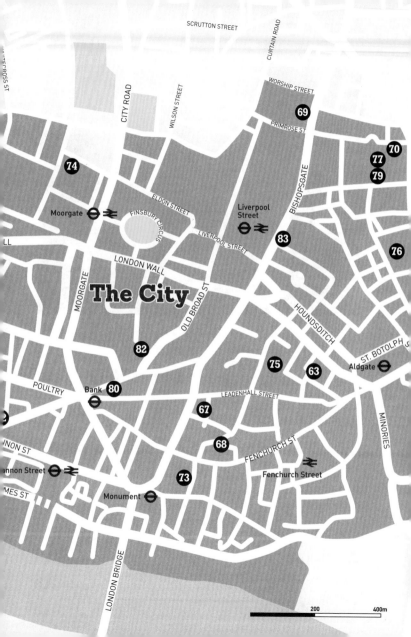

Alchemy Café

8 Ludgate Broadway, EC4V 6DU

The Alchemists of old attempted to transform ordinary materials into precious metals. This City café is well practiced in espresso alchemy; extracting liquid gold with an array of coffee apparatus, including a La Marzocco GB/5 and cold brew drip tower. The Alchemy wizards also operate a roastery in South London, which has earned a reputation as one of the capital's best up and coming roasters. Customers interested in delving deeper into the mysteries of espresso science should join one of Alchemy's coffee courses.

+44(0)20 7329 9904
www.alchemycoffee.co.uk
Blackfriars / City Thameslink Rail

MON-FRI. 7:00am - 5:00pm
SAT-SUN. Closed

First opened 2013
Roaster Alchemy Coffee
Machine La Marzocco GB/5, 2 groups
Grinder Mazzer Robur E x2, Mahlkönig EK 43

Espresso	£2.30
Cappuccino	£2.95
Latte	£2.95
Flat white	£2.75

MAP REF. 61

COFFEE 4.75 / 5

OVERALL 4.50 / 5 ★★★★⯪

Artigiano Espresso and Wine Bar

1 Paternoster Square, EC4M 7DX

A dual-level coffee and wine bar near St Paul's Cathedral, Artigiano attracts City workers seeking more than just a habitual caffeine hit. Coffee is sourced from highly regarded Cornish roaster Origin Coffee, and prepared by a well trained barista team on a La Marzocco Linea. Exposed brickwork and a contrasting grey and yellow design scheme create a striking backdrop. Go for lunch and you'll be hard pressed to resist the sandwiches, freshly prepared on-site with artisan bread.

+44(0)20 7248 0407
www.artigiano.uk.com
⊖ St Paul's

MON-TUE.	7:00am - 9:00pm
WED-FRI.	7:00am - 11:00pm
SAT-SUN.	10:30am - 6:00pm

First opened 2013
Roaster Origin Coffee Roasters
Machine La Marzocco Linea, 3 groups
Grinder Nuova Simonelli

Espresso	£2.00
Cappuccino	£2.70 / £2.95
Latte	£2.70 / £2.95
Flat white	£2.70

MAP REF.

COFFEE 4.25 / 5

OVERALL 4.50 / 5 ★★★★⯪

75

TOP 35

Association Coffee Creechurch Lane

10-12 Creechurch Lane, EC3A 5AY

Association brings gourmet coffee and quality food from small suppliers to the heart of the City. A meticulously prepared range of pastries, cakes and sandwiches are served in sleek but accessible surroundings. The interior follows a familiar industrial template while adding City-influenced twists including a tiled communal table studded with banker's lamps, offering a great spot for meetings or casual lunches. Association's brew bar should not be missed, manned by professional baristas who are serious about their craft.

+44(0)20 7283 1155
www.associationcoffee.com
⊖ Aldgate / Liverpool Street

Sister locations Ludgate Hill

MON-FRI.	7:30am – 5:00pm
SAT-SUN.	Closed

First opened 2012
Roaster Square Mile Coffee Roasters, Workshop Coffee and guests
Machine Synesso Hydra, 3 groups
Grinder Mahlkönig Peak

Espresso	£2.20
Cappuccino	£2.80
Latte	£2.80
Flat white	£2.80

MAP REF. **63**

COFFEE	OVERALL
4.75 / 5	4.75 / 5 ★★★★✦

Association Coffee Ludgate Hill

56 Ludgate Hill, EC4M 7AW

The City

This second branch of Association occupies a lovely space (dominated by pale wood in various guises) in a prime location, surrounded as it is by thirsty office workers. Popular within weeks of opening, the venue boasts not only two three-group Black Eagles but two Marco SP9s single-serve filter brewers to speed up service when things get busy. Espresso is as well made here as at the original in Creechurch Lane, with newspapers - plus a small food offering - serving the needs of those who want to linger.

+44(0)20 7283 1155
www.associationcoffee.com
City Thameslink / St Paul's / Blackfriars

Sister locations Creechurch Lane

MON-FRI.	7:30am - 5:00pm
SAT-SUN.	Closed

First opened 2015
Roaster Square Mile, Workshop Coffee and guests
Machine Victoria Arduino Black Eagle, 3 groups x2
Grinder Mahlkönig Peak

Espresso	£2.20
Cappuccino	£2.80
Latte	£2.80
Flat white	£2.80

MAP REF. **64**

COFFEE 4.50 / 5   OVERALL 4.50 / 5

77

Carter Lane Coffee House

50 Carter Lane, EC4V 5EA

Nestled in one of London's narrowest streets, this pint-sized coffee bar means business. Sitting proudly on the immaculate counter is a high end Synesso Hydra, operated by well-trained Italian baristas. A small selection of pastries and toasted sandwiches complement the coffee. The space may be small, but the lively staff create a convivial atmosphere in which to escape the city throng. Carter Lane successfully blends East End coffee expertise with a clean-cut style sharper than a city boy's lapels.

+44(0)20 7248 9493
www.carterlane-coffee.co.uk
⊖ St Paul's / ⇌ City Thameslink Rail

MON-FRI.	7:30am - 4:00pm
SAT-SUN.	Closed

First opened 2012
Roaster Climpson & Sons
Machine Synesso Hydra, 2 groups
Grinder Mazzer Robur x2, Mazzer Mini

Espresso	£1.70 / £2.00
Cappuccino	£2.60 / £2.90
Latte	£2.60 / £2.90
Flat white	£2.50

MAP REF. 65

COFFEE		OVERALL	
4.25 / 5		4.25 / 5	★★★★⯪

Chancery Press

81 Chancery Lane, WC2A 1DD

NEW

The first thing to be said about this lawyer-land branch of Press is that you won't find it where you'd expect to find it, unless you're familiar with the weird street-numbering in Chancery Lane. It's at the southern end, not the Holborn end. And it's worth finding. Apart from the always-well-made coffee there's a really pretty, quiet space, with high windows and a few places to perch in the pedestrian walkway running off of Chancery Lane. Drink the Caravan espresso blend with milk, or have a filter of exquisite quality made from beans roasted by Berlin's Barn roastery.

www.presscoffee.london
⊖ Chancery Lane

MON-FRI.	7:00am - 6:00pm
SAT-SUN.	Closed

First opened 2016
Roaster Caravan Coffee Roasters, The Barn
Machine La Marzocco Linea PB, 2 groups
Grinder Nuova Simonelli Mythos One

Espresso	£2.10
Cappuccino	£2.30
Latte	£2.30
Flat white	£2.60

Sister locations Fleet Street / St Bride

MAP REF. 66

COFFEE		OVERALL	
4.25 / 5		4.00 / 5	★★★★☆

The Coffee Works Project Leadenhall

Leadenhall Market, Whittington Avenue, EC3V 1PP

Diminutive size isn't always a handicap when it comes to coffee bars. But when the tiddler in question occupies prime real estate in the City with a massive customer base, there's a need to keep throughput of punters at a certain level. Within those limitations, however, Coffee Works Project Leadenhall is a dream come true. The clever use of chipboard as a decorative feature gives it a distinctive look, and the gourmet toasted sandwiches from former chef and owner Peter are superb. As is the coffee, of course: The Coffee Works Project, brewed on a Slayer V2.

+44(0)20 7621 0040
www.coffeeworksproject.com
⊖ Bank

MON-FRI.	7:30am – 5:00pm
SAT-SUN.	Closed

First opened 2015
Roaster The Coffee Works Project
Machine Slayer V2, 3 groups
Grinder Nuova Simonelli Mythos x2, Mahlkönig EK 43

Espresso	£2.20
Cappuccino	£2.80
Latte	£2.80
Flat white	£2.80

Sister locations Angel / Blackfriars Road

MAP REF. **67**

 COFFEE 4.50 / 5   **OVERALL 4.25 / 5** ★★★★⯪

Curators Coffee Studio

9a Cullum Street, EC3M 7JJ

There's a fine line between coffee and art at this small City café from former Kaffeine barista Catherine Seay. The vibrant turquoise La Marzocco Strada and matching grinders contrast with reclaimed wooden furniture and a vintage filing cabinet. The superb coffee is accompanied by irresistible cakes made in-house.

+44(0)20 7283 4642
www.curatorscoffee.com
⊖ Monument / Bank

Sister locations Curators Coffee Gallery

MON-FRI.	7:30am - 5:30pm
SAT-SUN.	Closed

First opened 2012
Roaster Local and international roasters
Machine La Marzocco Strada, 3 groups
Grinder Mazzer Robur E, Nuova Simonelli Mythos One, Anfim

Espresso	£2.20
Cappuccino	£2.80
Latte	£2.80
Flat white	£2.80

MAP REF. 68

COFFEE 4.50 / 5	OVERALL 4.50 / 5 ★★★★⯪

Department of Coffee and Social Affairs
Norton Folgate 201 Bishopgate, Norton Folgate, EC2M 3UG

Norton Folgate was a tiny self-governing area of East London that spanned just a few blocks up until 1855 and still gives its name to a short stretch of the A10. This narrow, sun-filled venue features a takeaway zone at one end and an eat-in area at the other. Custom-made lights inspired by the molecular structure of caffeine combine with a minimal black-and-white decor, high ceilings and huge windows to create a serene, crystalline space.

www.departmentofcoffee.com
⊖ Liverpool Street / Shoreditch High Street

Sister locations Spitalfields Market / Leather Lane / Carnaby Street / Piccadilly / Covent Garden

MON-FRI.	7:00am - 5:00pm
SAT-SUN.	Closed

First opened 2012
Roaster Department of Coffee and Social Affairs
Machine La Marzocco FB/80, 3 groups
Grinder Mazzer Robur E x2, Mazzer Super Jolly, Mahlkönig Tanzania

Espresso	£2.40
Cappuccino	£2.90
Latte	£2.90
Flat white	£3.00

MAP REF. 69

COFFEE 4.50 / 5	OVERALL 4.25 / 5 ★★★★⯪

Department of Coffee and Social Affairs

Spitalfields Market Spitalfields Arts Market, 6 Lamb Street, E1 6EA

Old Spitalfields Market has more coffee hangouts than ever, but there are still strong reasons to come here. You can watch the market crowds roll by from an outdoor seat or chill in the basement. Baked items provide a light lunch or afternoon sugar rush. But the main reason is the great coffee. It's all single-origin, with two espresso (one specifically for milky drinks) and one filter. The baristas combine the precision of scientists with the passion of lay preachers. Despite the competition, long queues prove that locals have got the message.

www.departmentofcoffee.com
⊖ Liverpool Street /
Shoreditch High Street

Sister locations Leather Lane / Norton Folgate / Carnaby Street / Piccadilly / Covent Garden

| MON-FRI. | 8:00am - 5:00pm |
| SAT-SUN. | 10:00am - 5:30pm |

First opened 2015
Roaster Department of Coffee and Social Affairs
Machine La Marzocco FB/80, 3 groups
Grinder Mazzer Super Jolly, Mazzer Robur E

Espresso	£2.40
Cappuccino	£2.70
Latte	£2.70
Flat white	£3.00

MAP REF. **70**

COFFEE 4.50 / 5 🫘🫘🫘🫘🫘

OVERALL 4.25 / 5 ★★★★⯪

Dose Espresso Barbican

70 Long Lane, EC1A 9EJ

Straddling the border between the City and Farringdon, Dose Espresso is recognised as a leader in London's artisanal coffee scene. Owner and barista James Phillips sets a high standard in his small but welcoming espresso bar. All Dose coffee, milk and ingredients are ethically sourced and environmental consciousness is an important part of the company's identity.

+44(0)20 7600 0382
www.dose-espresso.com
⊖ Barbican

MON-FRI.	7:00am – 5:00pm
SAT-SUN.	Closed

First opened 2009
Roaster Square Mile Coffee Roasters and guests
Machine Synesso Hydra, 3 groups
Grinder Ceado E92, Mahlkönig EK 43

Espresso	£2.00 / £2.20
Cappuccino	£2.90 / £3.30
Latte	£2.90 / £3.30
Flat white	£2.90 / £3.30

MAP REF. **71**

COFFEE 4.50 / 5

OVERALL 4.50 / 5 ★★★★⯪

Host

St Mary Aldermary Church, Watling Street, EC4M 9BW

Host may be the most tranquil place in the City of London that serves top-notch coffee - and perhaps the most heavenly, since it's inside a Gothic-revival church designed by Sir Christopher Wren. The City office workers who buy coffee here seem to love a quiet interlude in their working day. Coffee comes (appropriately) from Mission and is well made in double shots at reasonable prices. Food is minimal but you can bring in your own food if you buy a drink. And buying a 'caffe sospeso' (suspended coffee) will provide a hot drink for one of the local homeless people who come in regularly. Hallelujah!

+44(0)20 7248 9902
www.moot.uk.net/host
⊖ Mansion House

| MON-FRI. | 7:30am - 4:30pm |
| SAT-SUN. | Closed |

First opened 2012
Roaster Mission Coffee Works
Machine La Marzocco Linea, 2 groups
Grinder Mazzer Super Jolly

Espresso	£2.00
Cappuccino	£2.40
Latte	£2.60
Flat white	£2.40

MAP REF. 72

| COFFEE 4.25 / 5 | 🫘🫘🫘🫘◐ | OVERALL 4.25 / 5 | ★★★★✦ |

The New Black

10 Philpot Lane, EC3M 8AA

It's pretty much a dead cert that you've never seen a coffee bar that looks anything like The New Black. This London outpost of the original in Singapore is awash with lively, vivid colour. Polished steel gleams at the brewing stations, and there's a mural-size coffee flavour wheel on one wall. Nearly everything (including cups and furniture) has been designed for purpose. And if the look of the place is unique, so too is the coffee offering. First of all, there's not one house roaster but a raft of them, from all over the world. You'll have a choice of around a dozen coffees, divided between espresso-based and brewed. All are explaining stylistically on the wall menu, with excellent advice from the staff thrown in for nothing. If this sounds like a formula

for intimidating geekery, rest assured: some customers do want to go down that route, but others say 'I just want a coffee' and they are accommodated happily. Food is minimal and confined to sweet stuff, so this is not a place for mealtimes. The brewed coffees are stars here, especially when consumed in the elegant back room (or cute little courtyard in good weather). All in all, an exceptional addition to London's coffee scene. And in case you're wondering about the name, here's a clue: all the staff wear orange uniforms.

MAP REF. **73**

COFFEE 4.50 / 5	OVERALL 4.50 / 5 ★ ★ ★ ★ ★

The City

MON-FRI.	7:00am – 4:30pm
SAT.	11:00am – 4:00pm
SUN.	Closed

First opened 2016
Roaster Multiple roasters
Machine Modbar, 2 groups
Grinder Mahlkönig EK 43,
Nuova Simonelli Mythos One

Espresso	£2.80
Cappuccino	£3.10
Latte	£3.10
Flat white	£3.10

www.thenewblack.coffee
⊖ Monument

Notes Moorgate

CityPoint, 1 Ropemaker Street, EC2Y 9AW

Notes Moorgate suits drinkers whose coffee habit gradually transforms into a wine habit as day turns to night. When the coffee menu and wine list are as dependable as they are here, it's a habit to strive for if you ask us. The crescent-shaped space on the ground floor of the towering CityPoint building creates a breathtaking architectural backdrop to the sensory experience within. Notes has earned a hard-won reputation for sourcing and roasting excellent coffee, and this City location is the ideal setting to enjoy the fruits of the roaster's labour.

+44(0)20 7628 5175
www.notes-uk.co.uk
⊖ Moorgate

Sister locations Canary Wharf / Gherkin / King's Cross /Trafalgar Square

MON-WED.	7:00am - 9:00pm
THU-FRI.	7:00am - 10:00pm
SAT-SUN.	Closed

First opened 2014
Roaster Notes Coffee Roasters
Machine La Marzocco Linea PB, 2 groups x2
Grinder Nuova Simonelli Mythos x2, Mahlkönig EK 43

Espresso	£2.20	/ £2.40
Cappuccino	£2.70	/ £2.90
Latte	£2.70	/ £2.90
Flat white	£2.70	/ £2.90

MAP REF. **74**

COFFEE 4.50 / 5

OVERALL 4.50 / 5 ★★★★½

Notes The Gherkin

The Gherkin, 30 St Mary Axe, EC3A 8EP

 NEW

Notes has a knack for turning small, quirky spaces into distinctive dining and drinking destinations. This one at the base of the Gherkin is, like their King's Cross venue, on two levels. It's a very small space, but when you're sitting upstairs, size doesn't matter at all. Notes is a seriously good roaster, and drinks are of top quality whether from the La Marzocco or in filter. In the evening it turns into a wine bar with food. But not at weekends, when it's closed. This being the City and all.

+44(0)20 7283 2773
www.notes-uk.co.uk
⊖ Aldgate

Sister locations King's Cross / Moorgate / Trafalgar Square

MON-WED.	7:30am - 9:00pm
THU-FRI.	7:30am - 10:00pm
SAT-SUN.	Closed

First opened 2016
Roaster Notes Coffee Roasters
Machine La Marzocco Linea, 2 groups
Grinder Nuova Simonelli Mythos One

Espresso	£2.10
Cappuccino	£2.90
Latte	£2.90
Flat white	£2.90

MAP REF. **75**

COFFEE 4.25 / 5   **OVERALL** 4.00 / 5 ★ ★ ★ ★ ☆

Nude Coffee Roasters Bell Lane

8 Bell Lane, E1 7LA

The original Nude in Hanbury Street always seems to be heaving, but the newest addition to the stable is much smaller: there's seating for just 20 people at notably lovely tables. And with a smaller food offering (and no weekend opening), it's less neighbourhood hangout than a haven for local office workers. None of that detracts from the charms of this Nude. The coffee is made with the customary Nude Espresso Care and the gleaming Strada packs a nicely fruity kick. Sandwiches, salads and baked goods (all homemade) are attractively presented, and the service couldn't be friendlier.

www.nudeespresso.com
⊖ Aldgate East

Sister locations The Roastery (Hanbury St) / Hanbury St / Spitalfields Mkt

MON-FRI.	7:30am - 4:30pm
SAT-SUN.	Closed

First opened 2015
Roaster Nude Coffee Roasters
Machine La Marzocco Strada EE, 2 Groups
Grinder Nuovo Simonelli Mythos One x2, Compak K30

Espresso	£2.40
Cappuccino	£3.00
Latte	£3.00
Flat white	£3.00

MAP REF. **76**

COFFEE 4.50 / 5   **OVERALL** 4.25 / 5 ★ ★ ★ ★ ☆

Nude Espresso Spitalfields Market

Spitalfields Market, 4 Market Street, E1 6EW

Nude's most recent opening, in a big, high-ceilinged space on the south side of Old Spitalfields, competes against a number of other nearby coffee places - including another Nude just north of the market. But you should still expect to find it packed, even outside mealtimes. The Nude formula always works well, with a good brunch/lunch menu and excellent baked goods. And, of course, their fine beans brewed by skilled baristas. Don't neglect their pour-overs. And do grab a seat outside if weather permits, either before or after a stroll through the market.

www.nudeespresso.com
⊖ Aldgate East

Sister locations The Roastery (Hanbury St) / Hanbury Street / Bell Lane

MON-FRI. 7:30am - 5:30pm
SAT-SUN. 10:00am - 5:00pm

First opened 2016
Roaster Nude Coffee Roasters
Machine La Marzocco FB/80, 3 groups
Grinder Nuova Simonelli Mythos One, Mahlkönig K30

Espresso	£2.20
Cappuccino	£2.80
Latte	£2.80
Flat white	£2.80

MAP REF. **77**

COFFEE 4.25 / 5		OVERALL 4.25 / 5	★★★★⯪

Press Coffee & Co

3 Fleet Street, EC4Y 1AU

Press Coffee & Co (formerly named The Fleet Street Press) occupies a listed building complete with stunning stained glass window, and serves a mixed crowd of lawyers and students. Owners Davide Pastorino and Andy Wells oversee a friendly team pulling shots of Caravan coffee on a brand new La Marzocco. Expect top notch supplies including non-homogenised milk, and a healthy dose of witticisms dispensed to passers-by on what is surely London's most amusing pavement A-board sign.

+44(0)20 7583 7757
www.presscoffee.london
⊖ Temple

Sister locations Chancery Ln / Ludgate Circus

MON-FRI. 6:30am - 7:00pm
SAT-SUN. 9:00am - 6:00pm

First opened 2011
Roaster Caravan Coffee Roasters and guests
Machine La Marzocco Linea PB, 3 groups
Grinder Nuova Simonelli Mythos x2, Mazzer Mini, Mahlkönig Tanzania

Espresso	£2.10
Cappuccino	£2.40 / £2.70
Latte	£2.40 / £2.70
Flat white	£2.60

MAP REF. **78**

COFFEE 4.25 / 5		OVERALL 4.00 / 5	★★★★☆

Rapha Cycle Club Spitalfields Market

Old Spitalfields Market, 61-63 Brushfield Street, E1 6AA

You don't need to be a cycle-maniac to enjoy spending time with Rapha. They bring the same dedication to coffee and cooking as they bring to two-wheeled matters, hiring outstanding baristas and sourcing top-quality beans for serving from La Marzocco machines or in filters. There's not much in the way of seating inside, though there's extra outdoors for good weather. The location makes this a good place start (or end) an exploration of the market or of nearby Brick Lane. Despite the abundant competition, Rapha Cycle Club is a true local hero.

+44(0)20 7426 2000
pages.rapha.cc/clubs/spitalfields
◉ Liverpool Street

MON-FRI.	8:00am – 7:00pm
SAT.	9:00am – 7:00pm
SUN.	11:00am – 6:00pm

First opened 2015
Roaster Allpress Espresso
Machine La Marzocco Strada, 2 groups
Grinder Mazzer Kony E

Espresso	£2.30
Cappuccino	£3.00
Latte	£3.20
Flat white	£3.00

Sister locations Soho

MAP REF.

COFFEE
4.25 / 5

OVERALL
4.25 / 5 ★★★★⯪

Royal Exchange Grind

34 Royal Exchange, EC3V 3LP

No two Grinds are alike, but there's something special about this little branch in the Royal Exchange. You'll find crowds of caffeinistas coming for takeaways throughout the day, but the place is a very pleasant place to sit, too. And at 5pm on a Friday, you might well find a group of City gents sitting down for espresso Martinis rather than a plain old espresso. The food offering is Grind's usual delicious assortment of sandwiches and baked goods, and the staff are notably fun and friendly.

+44(0)20 3019 1807
grind.co.uk
⊖ Bank

Sister locations Clerkenwell / Covent Garden / Holborn / London Bridge / Shoreditch / Soho / Exmouth Market / Whitechapel

MON–FRI.	6:30am – 7:00pm
SAT–SUN.	Closed

First opened 2016
Roaster The Grind House Espresso
Machine La Marzocco Linea PB, 3 groups x2
Grinder Nuova Simonelli Mythos One x3, Mahlkönig Tanzania

Espresso	£2.30
Cappuccino	£2.90
Latte	£2.90
Flat white	£2.80

MAP REF. 80

COFFEE
4.25 / 5

OVERALL
4.25 / 5

Saint Bride Press

11 Saint Bride Street, EC4A 4AS

This newest Press location occupies a tiny space just off Ludgate Circus. Nearby office-bees rush in for al-desko brews, but there's seating for around a dozen people. For such a small space, St Bride creates a lively vibe. A dinky kitchen turns out breakfast, sandwiches, soups and stews. Baked goods beckon from the counter. Behind the bar, top-notch baristas produce shots from the gleaming Faema, best enjoyed with milk as always with Caravan's espresso blend. There are also excellent filtered brews made with beans from The Barn, in Berlin - top choice if you drink coffee black.

www.presscoffee.london
⊖ Blackfriars

MON-FRI.	6:30am - 6:30pm
SAT-SUN.	Closed

First opened 2016
Roaster Caravan Coffee Roasters, The Barn
Machine Faema E71
Grinder Nuova Simonelli Mythos One, Mazzer Mini

Espresso	£1.90
Cappuccino	£2.50
Latte	£2.50
Flat white	£2.60

Sister locations Chancery Lane / Fleet Street

MAP REF. **81**

Taylor St Baristas Bank

125 Old Broad Street, EC2N 1AR

This Bank venue is one of the largest and busiest cafés in the Taylor St Baristas family. The sleek and spacious design includes lofty ceilings, timber finishing, and designer drop lights. There's plenty of seating, making this a great place for a business meeting or lunchtime escape. Scrumptious lunch options are also on offer. The guest espresso changes every fortnight, and seasonal single origin coffees are served at the dedicated brew bar.

+44(0)20 7256 8665
www.taylor-st.com
Bank / Liverpool Street

Sister locations Liverpool Street / Shoreditch / Canary Wharf / Monument / Mayfair / South Quay / St Paul's

MON-FRI.	7:00am - 5:00pm
SAT-SUN.	Closed

First opened 2010
Roaster Taylor St Baristas
Machine Nuova Simonelli Aurelia II T3, 3 groups, Victoria Arduino White Eagle, 3 groups
Grinder Nuova Simonelli Mythos One x3, Anfim

Espresso	£2.00
Cappuccino	£2.80 / £3.20
Latte	£2.80 / £3.20
Flat white	£2.80 / £3.70

MAP REF.

COFFEE 4.50 / 5		OVERALL 4.50 / 5	

Taylor St Baristas Liverpool Street

1a New Street, EC2M 4TP

The City

The atmosphere at the smallest Taylor St venue is thick with intoxicating coffee aromas layered with heavy bass from the oversized soundsystem. The morning rush swells the narrow space, steam rolls and grinders spin up as the crack team of baristas perform in perfect synchrony, deftly working the queue to a quickening tempo. This accelerated coffee bar is a slingshot for the City's office workers, propelling them towards offices, meetings, and spreadsheets. It's a far cry from the larger Taylor St cafés, this store marches to an altogether different beat.

+44(0)20 7929 2207
www.taylor-st.com
⊖ Liverpool Street

Sister locations Bank / Canary Wharf / Monument / Mayfair / Shoreditch / South Quay / St Paul's

MON–FRI.	7:00am – 5:00pm
SAT–SUN.	Closed

First opened 2008
Roaster Taylor St Baristas
Machine Victoria Arduino Black Eagle, 3 groups, Victoria Arduino White Eagle, 2 groups
Grinder Anfim, Mazzer Robur, Mahlkönig Tanzania, Victoria Arduino Mythos One x2

Espresso	£2.00		
Cappuccino	£2.80 / £3.20 / £4.00		
Latte	£2.80 / £3.20 / £4.00		
Flat white	£2.80 / £3.70 / £4.40		

MAP REF. **83**

 COFFEE 4.50 / 5   OVERALL 4.00 / 5 ★★★★☆

93

EXCEPTIONAL
COFFEE

The fashionable boroughs of North London contain a huge variety of venues, from the colourful cafés of Camden – the rock 'n' roll hub of yesteryear – to chic neighbourhood delis in Islington. Moneyed Hampstead retains an English village style charm, just a short tube ride away from central London. Home to both busy professionals and counter-culture figures, the area's coffee culture reflects North London's diversity and fascinating history.

North

Beam

40-41 Topsfield Parade, N8 8PT

Sidar Akyuz, the Crouch End native who owns Beam, says that locals 'move to Shoreditch when they're 18 and move back here when they start a family.' Akyuz has catered for the local population brilliantly in this big, opulently gorgeous restaurant-café. If you're not eating, let yourself be guided to one of the 'comfy chairs', low and long enough to sleep in. Sweet things on the counter make a perfect partner for Allpress espresso brewed expertly in a three-group La Marzocco. This is a true local gem. Lucky Crouch End.

+44(0)20 8348 3748
www.cafebeam.co.uk
⊖ Finsbury Park

MON-SUN. 8:00am - 6:30pm

First opened 2013
Roaster Allpress Espresso
Machine La Marzocco Linea, 3 groups
Grinder Mazzer Robur, Mazzer Super Jolly

Espresso	£2.10
Cappuccino	£2.80
Latte	£2.80
Flat white	£2.80

MAP REF. **84**

Bear and Wolf

153 Fortress Road, NW5 2HR

Owner Matthew Neel planned B&W as a gathering place for parents with young children, right down to the playroom ('Cubroom') in back. Seating in the minimally decorated dining area comprises of a large window table, a counter opposite the serving area, and long, closely spaced reclaimed-wood tables in the back. The setup encourages conversation with your neighbours, and there is a winning community feel here. Well-made coffee from Ozone beans makes a fine conclusion to a light meal of notably good food, or a fitting companion to one of the home-baked pastries or cakes.

+44(0)20 3601 1900
www.bearandwolfcafe.com
⊖ Tufnell Park

MON-FRI.	7:30am - 5:30pm
SAT-SUN.	8:30am - 5:30pm

First opened 2014
Roaster Ozone Coffee Roasters
Machine La Marzocco Linea, 2 groups
Grinder Mazzer

Espresso	£2.00
Cappuccino	£2.75 / £3.25
Latte	£2.75 / £3.25
Flat white	£2.50

MAP REF. **85**

COFFEE 4.25 / 5

OVERALL 4.25 / 5 ★★★★✦

Bonjour Brioche

2a England's Lane, NW3 4TG

Bonjour Brioche is very popular with locals for its Monmouth coffee (expertly brewed daily to hit all the right sweet notes) and especially its excellent food. They make everything fresh, and even bake their own bagels and brioche of course. If you go for just one thing, go for something sweet: a slice of unfathomably moist, red velvet cake suggests that they have one of the best bakers in London. With notably friendly staff Bonjour Brioche is another local hero for the lucky inhabitants of Belsize Park.

+44(0)20 7846 0202
www.bonjourbrioche.co.uk
⊖ Chalk Farm

MON–FRI.	7:30am – 5:00pm
SAT–SUN.	8:00am – 5:00pm

First opened 2013
Roaster Monmouth Coffee
Machine La Marzocco FB, 2 groups
Grinder Mazzer Robur

Espresso	£2.20
Cappuccino	£2.70
Latte	£2.70
Flat white	£2.70

MAP REF. **86**

 COFFEE 4.25 / 5  OVERALL 4.50 / 5 ★★★★⯪

The Bowery Bagel Bakery

47 Chalk Farm Road, NW1 8AJ

Camden has long been a destination for exhilarating music, but its coffee scene has lagged behind its sister neighbourhoods like a woebegone groupie. The Bowery (formerly named Tower 47) is on a mission to put Camden back in the limelight. An ensemble of London's rockstar roasters grace the coffee menu, served with plenty of New York-style enthusiasm. The Bowery draws on a shared love of coffee, music, and the electric energy of Camden's streets.

+44(0)20 7482 2274
www.bbbcamden.co.uk
⊖ Chalk Farm

| MON-THU. | 9:00am - 4:00pm |
| SAT-SUN. | 7:30am - 10:00pm |

First opened 2013
Roaster Guest roasters
Machine La Spaziale S40, 3 groups
Grinder Mazzer Major, Mazzer Super Jolly, Ditting, Mahlkönig K30

Espresso	£2.10
Cappuccino	£2.70
Latte	£2.70
Flat white	£2.70

MAP REF. 87

| COFFEE 4.00 / 5 | | OVERALL 4.00 / 5 | ★★★★☆ |

Campbell & Syme

9 Fortis Green, N2 9JR

East Finchley may not be fashionable territory for a roastery café, but don't let this make you underestimate Campbell & Syme. The business was established by Joe Syme, an experienced hand in the catering sector, and Jon Cowell, a musician and long-time coffee aficionado. The team offer a variety of blends and single origins, and they have established direct relationships with individual producers, underlining their commitment to responsibly sourcing of top-quality coffee.

+44(0)7977 514 054
www.campbellandsyme.co.uk
⊖ East Finchley

| MON-FRI. | 7:30am - 5:00pm |
| SAT-SUN. | 9:00am - 5:00pm |

First opened 2013
Roaster Campbell & Syme
Machine La Marzocco Strada, 2 groups
Grinder Nuova Simonelli Mythos, Mahlkönig EK 43

Espresso	£2.20
Cappuccino	£2.80
Latte	£2.80
Flat white	£2.70

MAP REF. 88

| COFFEE 4.50 / 5 |  | OVERALL 4.25 / 5 | ★★★★⯪ |

Caravan King's Cross

1 Granary Square, N1C 4AA

Inhabiting a monolithic former granary building, Caravan is now firmly within the major league in both London's coffee and casual dining arenas. The unabashed use of concrete and other reclaimed materials create an industrial atmosphere on a grand scale. The knowledgeable baristas are happy to offer advice on their seasonal blends, which are freshly roasted on the premises. The worldly food menu and wide range of coffees offer an excellent opportunity to experiment with coffee and food pairings.

+44(0)20 7101 7661
www.caravankingscross.co.uk
🚇 King's Cross St Pancras

Sister locations Exmouth Market

MON-FRI.	8:00am - 11:30pm
SAT.	10:00am - 11:30pm
SUN.	10:00am - 4:00pm

First opened 2012
Roaster Caravan Coffee Roasters
Machine Faema E71, 3 groups
Grinder Mazzer Robur E x3,
Mahlkönig EK 43

Espresso	£2.00
Cappuccino	£2.60
Latte	£2.60
Flat white	£2.60

MAP REF. 89

COFFEE 5 / 5

OVERALL 5 / 5 ★★★★★

Coffee Circus

136 Crouch Hill, N8 9DX

With its circus theme and vintage tearoom feel, Coffee Circus is a friendly, whimsical place to discover. The café's hidden location seemingly cultivates the eccentricity and playfulness hidden within: it wouldn't surprise us if it concealed a cupboard with a portal to a fantasy-land. In addition to the well-poured coffee, expect a fanciful food menu including eggs and buttered soldiers. Coffee Circus transforms into an occasional evening performance space. The curious visitor is more likely to stumble upon jazz nights than performing elephants, but one can always hope.

+44(0)20 8340 8221
www.coffeecircus.co.uk
⊖ Crouch Hill

| MON-FRI. | 8:00am - 6:00pm |
| SAT-SUN. | 9:00am - 6:00pm |

First opened 2010
Roaster Mission Coffee Works, Campbell & Syme
Machine La Marzocco Linea PB, 2 groups
Grinder Mazzer Robur E, Ditting, Nuova Simonelli Mythos Clima Pro, Sage Pro

Espresso	£2.00
Cappuccino	£2.60
Latte	£2.60
Flat white	£2.60

MAP REF. **90**

COFFEE 4.25 / 5

OVERALL 4.25 / 5 ★★★★✬

The Coffee Jar

83 Parkway, NW1 7PP

If you're a newcomer, you may be greeted with the words 'Is this your first time here?' or something along those lines. Coffee Jar has been trading in this minute spot since 2013, and most people are regulars. It's easy to see why. Monmouth beans are brewed with exceptional care, food is good and well-priced (try a chocolate chip cookie), and the welcome is naturally warm. There's little seating, so be prepared to wait if you want to get comfortable. An independent gem in a part of north London that's seeing lots of chains move in.

www.thecoffeejar.co.uk
⊖ Camden Town

MON–FRI.	7:30am – 5:30pm
SAT–SUN.	9:00am – 5:30pm

First opened 2013
Roaster Monmouth Coffee Company
Machine La Marzocco Linea, 2 groups
Grinder Mazzer Robur E

Espresso	£2.00
Cappuccino	£2.60
Latte	£2.70
Flat white	£2.60

MAP REF.

 COFFEE 4.00 / 5   **OVERALL** 4.00 / 5

The Coffee Works Project Angel

96-98 Islington High Street, N1 8EG

The Coffee Works Project owner Peter Theoklitou comes from a family of chefs and it shows. This stunning venue offers top-quality coffee and a fine deli menu. The centrepiece of the café is a beautiful Seattle-made Slayer espresso machine - the first of its kind in London. A variety of house seasonal roasts are available as espresso and on filter, complemented by a range of British cheeses and charcuterie. The Coffee Works Project is now an integral player within the London coffee scene and a must-visit destination.

+44(0)20 7424 5020
www.coffeeworksproject.com
⊖ Angel

Sister locations Leadenhall / Blackfriars Road

MON-FRI.	7:30am - 6:00pm
SAT.	9:00am - 6:00pm
SUN.	10:00am - 5:00pm

First opened 2012
Roaster The Coffee Works Project
Machine Slayer V3, 3 groups
Grinder Nuova Simonelli Mythos x2, Mahlkönig EK 43

Espresso	£2.20
Cappuccino	£2.80
Latte	£2.80
Flat white	£2.80

MAP REF. **92**

COFFEE 4.50 / 5

OVERALL 4.75 / 5 ★★★★★

103

Cricks Corner

80 Dartmouth Park Hill, N19 5HU

Some coffee places have nothing that's close to wow-factor yet still make a big impression. Crick's Corner is one of them. Set in two tiny rooms on a corner site, it offers a small selection of sandwiches and baked goods - all of very high quality. The barista skills do full justice to Climpson's beans. The front room is where people seem to socialise, while in back there's a little lending library and sheets of paper for the kiddies to draw on. This quiet neighbourhood, far from the nearest tube, is lucky to have Cricks in its midst.

⊖ Archway

MON-FRI.	8:00am - 4:00pm
SAT-SUN.	9:00am - 3:00pm

First opened 2015
Roaster Climpson & Sons
Machine La Marzocco FB/80, 3 groups
Grinder Nuova Simonelli Mythos One, Mahlkönig K30

Espresso	£2.00
Cappuccino	£2.50
Latte	£2.50
Flat white	£2.40

MAP REF.

 COFFEE 4.00 / 5

 OVERALL 3.75 / 5 ★★★½☆

The Fields Beneath

52a Prince of Wales Road, NW5 3LN

Named after Gillian Tindall's 1977 historical study of Kentish Town, this small speciality coffee outpost has rallied a loyal local following. Owned by long-time coffee aficionado Gavin Fernback, the converted railway arch at Kentish Town West station is a small but attractive coffee bar. Railway arches are often dark and rather forbidding sites, but nothing could be further from the truth here. The space is bathed in floods of light, illuminating the bare brick walls and the counter's intricate Moroccan-style tiling. This place is soon turning vegan. Watch this space.

+44(0)20 7424 8838
⊖ Kentish Town West

MON-FRI.	7:00am - 4:00pm
SAT.	8:00am - 5:00pm
SUN.	9:00am - 5:00pm

First opened 2012
Roaster Fields Beneath Coffee and guests
Machine La Marzocco Linea, 2 groups
Grinder Nuova Simonelli Mythos

Espresso	£2.00
Cappuccino	£2.60
Latte	£2.70
Flat white	£2.60

MAP REF. **94**

COFFEE
4.50 / 5

OVERALL
4.25 / 5 ★★★★⯪

Fink's Salt and Sweet

70 Mountgrove Road, N5 2LT

Fink's is a shop, deli, café, restaurant. Above all else, however, it's an exemplary neighbourhood hangout. Mealtimes can be mental, especially at weekends, but out of peak hours it's great for mums with babies, laptop users, friends meeting for coffee and a chat. The big front room is best for socialising, the nook at the back for working. Beans from Caravan call out for milk, perhaps with something gluten-free (there's a good selection) on the side. Locals have been keeping Fink's busy since the day it opened; they know a good thing when they see it.

020 7684 7189
finks.co.uk
⊖ Arsenal

MON-WED.	9:00am - 7:00pm
THU.	9:00am - 10:30pm
FRI-SAT.	9:00am - 11:00pm
SUN.	10:00am - 5:00pm

First opened 2014
Roaster Caravan Coffee Roasters
Machine La Marzocco Linea, 2 groups
Grinder Mazzer Major

Espresso	£2.00
Cappuccino	£2.60
Latte	£2.60
Flat white	£2.60

MAP REF. **95**

COFFEE 4.00 / 5

OVERALL 4.25 / 5 ★★★★

Ginger & White Belsize Park

2 England's Lane, NW3 4TG

Larger than its sister shop in Hampstead, Ginger & White Belsize Park was something of a happy accident - owners Tonia, Nicholas and Emma simply couldn't resist the high-ceilinged, sun-drenched corner venue when it became available. The café's kitchen supplies food to both Ginger & White stores. The large communal table is well-stocked with homemade peanut butter and preserves, while the cute upstairs area and outdoor tables are ideal spots to tuck into the moreish sandwiches and decadent cakes.

+44(0)20 7722 9944
www.gingerandwhite.com
⊖ Chalk Farm / Belsize Park

Sister locations Hampstead

| MON-FRI. | 7:30am - 5:30pm |
| SAT-SUN. | 8:30am - 5:30pm |

First opened 2012
Roaster Square Mile Coffee Roasters
Machine La Marzocco FB/80, 3 groups
Grinder Nuova Simonelli Mythos One

Espresso	£2.50
Cappuccino	£3.25
Latte	£3.25
Flat white	£3.25

MAP REF. **96**

COFFEE
4.50 / 5

OVERALL
4.25 / 5 ★★★★⯪

Ginger & White Hampstead

4a-5a Perrin's Court, NW3 1QS

This proudly British café wears its heart on its sleeve. A local gem that is ever popular with the Hampstead community, Ginger & White serves well-crafted Square Mile coffee alongside modern British meals, made using locally sourced produce. With the choice of a communal dining table, window seats, or intimate leather sofas, this is a great place to enjoy a leisurely brunch.

+44(0)20 7431 9098
www.gingerandwhite.com
Hampstead

Sister locations Belsize Park

| MON-FRI. | 7:30am - 5:30pm |
| SAT-SUN. | 8:30am - 5:30pm |

First opened 2009
Roaster Square Mile Coffee Roasters
Machine La Marzocco FB/80, 3 groups
Grinder Nuova Simonelli Mythos One

Espresso	£2.50
Cappuccino	£3.25
Latte	£3.25
Flat white	£3.25

MAP REF.

COFFEE
4.50 / 5

OVERALL
4.25 / 5
★★★★✬

Granger & Co King's Cross

Stanley Building, 7 Pancras Square, N1C 4AG

The area around King's Cross is hardly short of places to eat and drink, but Granger is deservedly popular. This is a lovely space, like all Granger restaurants, with huge windows that give an ample view of the throngs passing by. Most people come for a meal from their Australia-derived all-day menus. Others come and sit at the bar for a coffee and a scrumptious cake or pastry. Espresso-based drinks are well made, and plenty of people come in for something milky to take to the office, but the real star is the cold drip.

MON-FRI.	7:00am - 11:00pm
SAT.	9:00am - 11:00pm
SUN.	10:00am - 6:00pm

First opened 2014
Roaster Allpress Espresso
Machine La Marzocco Linea AV, 3 groups
Grinder Mazzer Robur, Mazzer Super Jolly

+44(0)20 3058 2567
grangerandco.com
🔴 King's Cross

Sister locations Clerkenwell / Notting Hill

Espresso	£2.80
Cappuccino	£2.80
Latte	£2.80
Flat white	£2.80

MAP REF. **98**

COFFEE 4.25 / 5	OVERALL 4.25 / 5 ★★★★☆

Harris + Hoole Crouch End

9 The Broadway, N8 8DU

This branch of Harris + Hoole, a perfect fit with Crouch End, attracts a varied crowd. The long, attractive space has well-spaced seating on either chairs and sofas, and there's table space for workers with laptops. Coffee is expertly made on the three-group Simonelli, though there's also a choice of filter methods for single-origin beans. The word 'friendly' doesn't begin to describe the welcome here - so it's hardly surprising that the place is full of regulars.

MON-FRI.	7:00am - 6:00pm
SAT.	8:30am - 6:00pm
SUN.	9:00am - 5:00pm

First opened 2013
Roaster Harris + Hoole
Machine Nuova Simonelli Aurelia, 3 groups
Grinder Nuova Simonelli Mythos One, Mahlkönig Tanzania

+44(0)20 8347 6269
www.harrisandhoole.co.uk
🔴 Archway

Sister locations Tooley Street / Kensington / Imperial Wharf / Fulham

Espresso	£1.80
Cappuccino	£2.50
Latte	£2.50
Flat white	£2.50

MAP REF. **99**

COFFEE 4.25 / 5	OVERALL 4.25 / 5 ★★★★☆

Lantana Camden

Camden Market, Camden Lock Place, NW1 8AF

After the success of Lantana Fitzrovia and Shoreditch, the Australian team established this café in the heart of lively Camden Lock Market. Formerly named Ruby Dock, this café adds to the appeal of the area by bringing in specialty coffee and delicious small plates and cakes. It's an excellent place to catch a quick caffeine fix, rest weary feet, and get some respite from the crowds. If you're in the mood for something stronger, the baristas will happily fix you a cocktail.

+44(0)20 7428 0421
Camden Town

Sister locations Fitzrovia / Shoreditch

MON-SUN.   8:00am - 5:00pm

First opened 2013
Roaster Alchemy bespoke blend
Machine La Marzocco Linea, 2 groups
Grinder Mazzer Robur E, Mazzer Super Jolly

Espresso	£2.20
Cappuccino	£2.80
Latte	£2.80
Flat white	£2.80

MAP REF. **100**

COFFEE 4.25 / 5

OVERALL 4.00 / 5 ★★★★☆

Leyas

20 Camden High Street, NW1 0JH

Camden High Street has long been the domain of coffee chain outlets, but this independent provides a welcome alternative. The spacious downstairs area is decorated with artwork and murals, and offers plenty of seating with mismatched tables and inviting chesterfield sofas. Leyas has upped the ante in NW1 when it comes to coffee, offering up beans from Mission. Leyas is also an excellent place to enjoy a leisurely brunch, served every day until noon, and until 3:30pm on weekends.

www.leyas.co.uk
 Mornington Crescent

| MON-FRI. | 7:30am – 6:00pm |
| SAT-SUN. | 9:00am – 6:00pm |

First opened 2011
Roaster Mission Coffee Works
Machine La Marzocco GB/5, 2 groups
Grinder Nuova Simonelli Mythos One, Mahlkönig EK 43

Espresso	£2.20
Cappuccino	£2.60 / £2.80
Latte	£2.60 / £2.80
Flat white	£2.60

MAP REF. **101**

COFFEE 4.25 / 5   **OVERALL** 4.25 / 5 ★★★★⯪

Local Blend

587 Green Lanes, N8 0RG

Like an oasis in a desert of Turkish kebab houses and convenience stores, Local Blend finally brings speciality coffee to Harringay. The spacious Danish-inspired café feels like a living room, with comfy armchairs dotted around and a magazine stand overflowing with good reads. Owners Steve Talevski and Linda Zubairi make you feel as if they are welcoming you into their own home. Climpson & Sons coffee, brunch, and an array of sweet treats are served during the day.

+44(0)20 8341 2939
www.localblend.co.uk
 Turnpike Lane / Harringay Green Lanes

Sister locations Notting Hill

MON-FRI.	8:30am – 5:00pm
SAT.	9:30am – 5:00pm
SUN.	10:00am – 5:00pm

First opened 2013
Roaster Climpson & Sons
Machine La Marzocco Linea PB, 3 groups
Grinder Mazzer Super Jolly, Mazzer Mini, Ditting

Espresso	£1.90
Cappuccino	£2.50
Latte	£2.50
Flat white	£2.50

MAP REF. **102**

COFFEE 4.25 / 5    **OVERALL** 4.25 / 5 ★★★★⯪

Loft Coffee Company

4 Canfield Gardens, NW6 3BS

What Loft lacks in space, it compensates for with exceptionally friendly service, a welcome remedy to the scrum of Finchley Road. Sung-Jae Lee and his wife have created an uncomplicated, whitewashed space with warm wood panelling and a small number of tables. The Monmouth coffee is complemented by guest espresso such as Square Mile 'Red Brick'. Serving reliably excellent brews in an area not known for speciality coffee, Loft is a blessing for locals in search of a quality cup.

+44(0)20 7372 2008
🚇 Finchley Road

MON-FRI.	7:00am – 5:00pm
SAT.	8:00am – 4:00pm
SUN.	10:00am – 3:00pm

First opened 2012
Roaster Monmouth Coffee Company and guests
Machine La Marzocco Linea PB, 3 groups
Grinder Mazzer Kold

Espresso	£2.30
Cappuccino	£2.70
Latte	£2.70
Flat white	£2.70

MAP REF. **103**

COFFEE 4.25 / 5	OVERALL 4.25 / 5

Maison d'Etre Coffee House

154 Canonbury Road, N1 2UP

This pretty café on the Highbury roundabout is a labour of love for owners Kim and Kostas, who gave up their day jobs to pursue a passion for food and coffee. Maison d'Etre serves a range of homemade cakes, sandwiches, treats, and weekend brunch to an enthusiastic local crowd. Carefully selected artisan suppliers, hand-painted murals, vintage china, and a welcoming atmosphere make this a serene spot to take five in, particularly during the summer in the conservatory.

+44(0)20 7226 4711
www.maisondetrecafe.co.uk
🚇 Highbury & Islington

| MON-FRI. | 7:30am – 6:00pm |
| SAT-SUN. | 10:00am – 5:00pm |

First opened 2011
Roaster Square Mile Coffee Roasters
Machine La Marzocco Linea, 2 groups
Grinder Mazzer Major, Mazzer Super Jolly

Espresso	£2.10
Cappuccino	£2.80
Latte	£2.80
Flat white	£2.80

MAP REF. **104**

COFFEE 4.00 / 5	OVERALL 4.00 / 5

Melrose and Morgan Primrose Hill

42 Gloucester Avenue, NW1 8JD

This grocer and deli in leafy Primrose Hill is a cornucopia of beautifully prepared, locally sourced food. Homemade preserves fill the shelves, alongside a daily selection of seasonal salads, sandwiches, soups, and breads. Enjoy your coffee in the relaxing seating area while contemplating the irresistible range of cakes, tarts, and tray bakes. Melrose and Morgan is one of London's very best purveyors of artisan produce, recognised with two 'Great Taste' awards.

+44(0)20 7722 0011
www.melroseandmorgan.com
⊖ Chalk Farm / Camden Town

Sister locations Hampstead

MON-FRI.	8:00am - 7:00pm
SAT.	8:00am - 6:00pm
SUN.	9:00am - 5:00pm

First opened 2004
Roaster Mission Coffee Works
Machine La Marzocco Linea, 2 groups
Grinder Anfim

Espresso	£1.95
Cappuccino	£2.60
Latte	£2.60
Flat white	£2.60

MAP REF. **105**

COFFEE 4.00 / 5   OVERALL 4.00 / 5 ★★★★☆

Nanna's

274b St Paul's Road, N1 2LJ

It's hard not to smile when you walk through Nanna's door. The room is not particularly small, but it feels intimate and domestic. And that's intentional, because owner Sally Stall set out to evoke a 1970s feel, like her Nanna's front room to be precise. Choose between sofas and tables for seating, and tuck into fairly priced sandwiches and pastries. Vagabond coffee is on standby and is handled with true respect. Nanna's has 'the same faces' coming in throughout the week. You can't blame the locals for loving this place.

+44(0)20 7998 8686
www.nannasn1.com
⊖ Highbury & Islington

MON-WED. 8:00am - 9:00pm
THU-FRI. 8:00am - Late
SAT. 9:00am - Late
SUN. 9:00am - 9:00pm

First opened 2014
Roaster Vagabond Coffee
Machine La Marzocco Linea, 2 groups
Grinder Mazzer Super Jolly

Espresso	£1.80 / £2.00
Cappuccino	£2.70
Latte	£2.60
Flat white	£2.70

MAP REF. 106

COFFEE
4.00 / 5

OVERALL
4.25 / 5
★★★★

Notes King's Cross

Unit 2, One Pancras Square, N1C 4AG

Notes has struck just the right chord with this branch. The office complexes around King's Cross are not exactly over-filled with cosy hangouts, but Notes manages it surprisingly well on two floors, a ground floor and mezzanine with total capacity of around 35. Notes' in-house roasting has gone from strength to strength, and a changing roster of single-origin espressos includes some unusual lots handled with skill. The food offer is smaller in range than at other branches, but there's enough to keep the place busy when it turns into a wine bar at 5pm.

+44(0)20 7628 5175
www.notes-co.uk
⊖ King's Cross St Pancras

Sister locations Canary Wharf / Gherkin / Moorgate / Trafalgar Square

MON-TUE.	7:30am - 9:00pm
WED-FRI.	7:30am - 10:00pm
SAT.	10:00am - 5:30pm
SUN.	10:30am - 5:30pm

First opened 2015
Roaster Notes Coffee Roasters and guests
Machine La Marzocco Linea PB, 2 groups x2
Grinder Nuova Simonelli Mythos x2, Mahlkönig EK 43

Espresso	£2.20 / £2.40
Cappuccino	£2.70 / £2.90
Latte	£2.70 / £2.90
Flat white	£2.70 / £2.90

MAP REF. **107**

COFFEE 4.25 / 5

OVERALL 4.25 / 5 ★★★★⯪

Origin Coffee Roasters British Library

British Library, 96 Euston Road, NW1 2DB

It's temptingly easy for great public institutions such as libraries and museums to settle for the 'good enough' approach to casual catering, and many of them do just that. The British Library took a different route when it gave the franchise for its café to Origin. That should really be *cafés*: there are two separate Origin spaces here, and they couldn't be more different.

One, the first to open, is in the right-hand side of the airy foyer of the main library building. Though it's for takeaway-only in principle (expect paper cups), the library has put in tables and chairs so you can sit and talk or read. There always seem to be people doing just that, with or without a cake or pastry. The other space is a snug

sliver of a room with a big window and stools overlooking Euston Road. There's a bit more food on offer here, and the sandwiches are nice-looking.

Origin trains its baristas very well, and the single-origin batch brews are as much of a draw as espresso-based brews. Perch here a while and watch life pass by on Euston Road (or sit outside if the fumes don't defeat you). This is a small place of mega quality. Full marks to the Library for inviting Origin to this great learning institution.

MAP REF. **108**

COFFEE 4.50 / 5	OVERALL 4.25 / 5

116

MON–FRI.	7:00am – 6:00pm
SAT.	9:30am – 5:00pm
SUN.	11:00am – 5:00pm

Sister locations Hammersmith /
Shoreditch

First opened 2016
Roaster Origin Coffee Roasters
Machine Spirit Triplette, 3 groups
Grinder Mahlkönig EK 43,
Nuova Simonelli Mythos One

Espresso	£2.20
Cappuccino	£2.80
Latte	£2.80
Flat white	£2.60

www.origincoffee.co.uk
 King's Cross

Ripe Kitchen

136 Regents Park Road, NW1 8XL

This friendly Primrose Hill local does everything right. It's a lovely place to sit, and serves food from breakfast onwards - which makes it a shame just to order takeaway, as many customers do. (Though weekends are very busy, in case you're looking for brunch.) In addition to the Antipodean-inspired brunch offer, Ripe offers a soup of the day and a stew of the day, at prices that are extremely reasonable for such an upscale location. Ripe Kitchen's rendition of Square Mile espresso brings out all its rounded fruity notes. And this little gem even has its own blends of tea.

www.ripekitchen.co.uk
⊖ Chalk Farm

MON-FRI.	7:30am - 5:00pm
SAT.	8:00am - 5:30pm
SUN.	8:30am - 5:30pm

First opened 2014
Roaster Square Mile Coffee Roasters
Machine La Marzocco GB5, 2 groups
Grinder Macap MXD Xtreme, Mazzer Super Jolly

Espresso	£2.20
Cappuccino	£2.70
Latte	£2.70
Flat white	£2.60

MAP REF. **109**

COFFEE 4.25 / 5

OVERALL 4.25 / 5 ★★★★✩

Saint Espresso

Angel House, 26 Pentonville Road, N1 9HJ

Saint Espresso says a lot about the status of coffee in London today. Aptly named due to its location in Angel House, Saint's interior is clean and understated. The elegant branding and subtle lighting creates a refined ambiance. The service is attentive and the baristas direct the attention of the curious customer towards tasting notes for the various beans on offer. If it wasn't for the espresso machine and retail display of coffee home brewing gear, this could just as easily be an upscale wine bar. Saint extolls the virtues of the cult of espresso, and Londoners are converting in droves.

www.saintespresso.com

 Angel

MON-FRI.   7:30am - 6:00pm
SAT-SUN.   9:00am - 6:00pm

First opened 2014
Roaster Rotating roasters
Machine La Marzocco Strada, 2 groups
Grinder Mahlkönig EK 43,
Nuova Simonelli Mythos One

Espresso	£2.20
Cappuccino	£2.70
Latte	£2.70
Flat white	£2.70

MAP REF. 110

COFFEE 4.50 / 5   **OVERALL** 4.50 / 5 ★★★★⯪

Sawyer & Gray

290 St Paul's Road, N1 2LH

'We wanted it to be a nice place for everyone.' That's how the owners describe their goal here, and with a constant flow of customers, they must be doing something right. The interior could be described as 'quirky brilliance'. Climpson's beans get the full respect and the food covers lots of bases, from breakfast and brunch basics to more adventurous cooking in the evening.

+44(0)20 3417 5950
www.sawyerandgray.co.uk
Highbury & Islington

MON.	7:30am – 3:00pm
TUE.	Closed
WED-FRI.	7:30am – 3:00pm
SAT.	8:30am – 4:00pm
SUN.	9:30am – 4:00pm

First opened 2015
Roaster Climpson & Sons and guests
Machine La Marzocco GB5, 2 groups
Grinder Mazzer Major, Mazzer Super Jolly

Espresso	£2.20
Cappuccino	£2.50
Latte	£2.50
Flat white	£2.50

MAP REF. 111

COFFEE 4.00 / 5 OVERALL 4.25 / 5 ★★★★☆

Sunday

169 Hemingford Road, N1 1DA

Sunday is the place you daydream about on a sullen Monday morning. Snuggled on a residential street in Barnsbury, this tiny neighbourhood café aims to make every day feel like a weekend. It's a glowing composition of cappuccinos, broadsheets, broad smiles, pancakes, and imaginative egg dishes. Everything here comes together for beauty and good: the Caravan coffee is made with care and the brunch is one of the best in London. Sunday truly is a victory over the week gone by, but be prepared to queue.

+44(0)20 7607 3868

Caledonian Road & Barnsbury / Highbury & Islington

MON.	Closed
TUE-FRI.	8:30am – 6:00pm
SAT-SUN.	9:00am – 6.00pm

First opened 2013
Roaster Caravan Coffee Roasters
Machine La Marzocco Linea, 2 groups
Grinder Mazzer Super Jolly

Espresso	£2.30
Cappuccino	£2.90 / £3.30
Latte	£2.90 / £3.30
Flat white	£2.90 / £3.30

MAP REF. 112

COFFEE 4.00 / 5 OVERALL 4.25 / 5 ★★★★☆

Tintico

2-4 Station Road, N3 2SP

Tintico is just a two-minute walk from Finchley Central tube, so it's a perfect place to pitch up for the pre-commute pick-me-up. But those who stay a while are those get the full benefit of this lovely, lively local. It's on a corner site with big windows that let in lots of light even on a dull day. Service is warm and efficient, sandwiches are tasty. As are the well-made brews pulled through their three-group La Marzocco. And if you're a fan of the blues, you'll love what's on the sound system.

tinti.co

⊖ Finchley Central

MON-FRI.	7:00am – 5:30pm
SAT.	9:00am – 5:30pm
SUN.	10:00am – 5:30pm

First opened 2014
Roaster Campbell & Syme
Machine La Marzocco GB5, 3 groups
Grinder Mazzer Robur

Espresso	£1.80
Cappuccino	£2.40
Latte	£2.60
Flat white	£2.40

MAP REF. **113**

COFFEE
4.25 / 5

OVERALL
4.00 / 5 ★★★★★

121

Vagabond N4

Charter Court, Stroud Green Road, N4 3SG

Vagabond N4 brings top-quality coffee to the otherwise sleepy Crouch Hill. The interior is artfully constructed with recycled wood and coffee sacks, while the coffee bar is manned by a team of extremely friendly and passionate baristas. In addition to espresso-based coffee, the café offers Sandows Cold Brew (Sandows operates its brewing operation in the basement of the Vagabond store on Holloway Road). A small number of tables outside offer the perfect spot to enjoy this refreshing caffeine beverage on a nice sunny day.

+44(0)7527 049 414
www.vagabond.coffee
⊖ Finsbury Park / Crouch Hill

Sister locations Vagabond N7 / Vagabond E1 / Vagabond at Trade Union / Charlotte St

| MON-FRI. | 7:00am - 7:00pm |
| SAT-SUN. | 7:00am - 6:00pm |

First opened 2012
Roaster Vagabond Coffee Roasters
Machine Nuova Simonelli Aurelia II, 3 groups
Grinder Compak E8, Anfim

Espresso	£2.00
Cappuccino	£2.50 / £2.70
Latte	£2.50 / £2.70
Flat white	£2.50

MAP REF. 114

COFFEE 4.50 / 5 OVERALL 4.25 / 5 ★★★★

Vagabond N7

105 Holloway Road, N7 8LT

TOP 35

With this second venue, the Vagabond boys have perfected the deliberately unfinished interior look. The pockmarked walls and weathered wooden floorboards create a delightfully grungy vibe, and the enormous back room is home to an impressive Giesen roaster. There's also an inviting, if somewhat ramshackle, rear garden. The coffee is made with exceptional care, and single origins are available brewed by AeroPress or V60. Vagabond is an energetic, young coffee business with a roasting operation that promises to offer some excellent new coffees this year.

www.vagabond.coffee
⊖ Highbury & Islington

North

MON-FRI. 7:30am - 5:00pm
SAT-SUN. 9:00am - 6:00pm

First opened 2013
Roaster Vagabond Coffee Roasters
Machine Conti Monte Carlo, 3 groups
Grinder Compak R120, Compak E8

Espresso £2.00
Cappuccino £2.60 / £3.10
Latte £2.60 / £3.10
Flat white £2.60

Sister locations Vagabond N4 / Vagabond E1 / Trade Union / Charlotte St   MAP REF. 115

| COFFEE 4.50 / 5 | OVERALL 4.50 / 5 ★★★★⯪ |

Velasquez and Van Wezel

78 Park Road, N8 8JQ

NEW

There's a kind of stripped-back simplicity about Velasquez and Van Wezel. It's a smallish space dominated by a huge window, with little seating and just a few sandwiches and baked goodies to eat. The one thing that's huge is coffee quality, from a custom-built Kees van der Westen or filters. The owners grew up in the coffee business and they handle Square Mile's beans with consummate skill. But they also know how to make even a simple space into a warm and welcoming hangout, both for locals and for those coming in to enjoy the area's attractions.

+44(0)7715 881 949
www.velasquezandvanwezel.co.uk
⊖ Archway

MON-FRI. 7:30am - 5:00pm
SAT-SUN. 8:30am - 5:00pm

First opened 2016
Roaster Square Mile Coffee Roasters
Machine Kees van der Westen
Grinder Nuova Simonelli Mythos One, Mahlkönig EK 43

Espresso £2.00
Cappuccino £2.70
Latte £2.50
Flat white £2.50

MAP REF. 116

| COFFEE 4.25 / 5 | OVERALL 4.00 / 5 ★★★★☆ |

Wired Co.

194 Broadhurst Gardens, NW6 3AY

After a short stint on West End Lane, Wired found its permanent home on nearby Broadhurst Gardens. Bare steel, reclaimed wood, and industrial fittings create an austere first impression, but settle in with a brew and the atmosphere is soon enriched by the chocolaty notes of Climpson & Sons coffee. If sweet things are your weakness, you'll find plenty to tempt you, including lemon and poppy seed cakes from The Flour Station bakery. Thankfully for West Hampstead locals, this Wired is now a local institution.

West Hampstead

Sister locations Cable Co.

MON–FRI.	7:30am – 5:00pm
SAT–SUN.	9:00am – 5:00pm

First opened 2013
Roaster Climpson & Sons and guest roasters
Machine La Marzocco Linea, 2 groups
Grinder Nuova Simonelli Mythos One, Mazzer Major E, Mazzer Mini, Anfim

Espresso	£2.10
Cappuccino	£2.70
Latte	£2.70
Flat white	£2.60

MAP REF. 117

COFFEE 4.25 / 5

OVERALL 4.25 / 5 ★★★★☆

GET 'EM ALL

29 teas in all shapes and sizes

DISCOVER MORE and **SHOP ONLINE** at
teapigs.co.uk

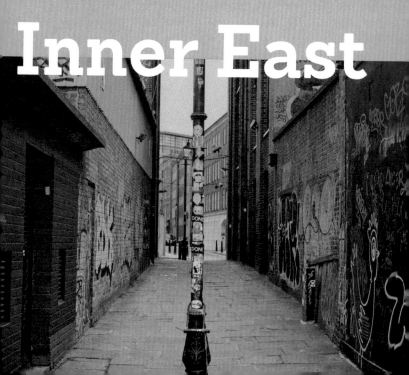

Brick Lane and Shoreditch provide London's creative pulse and are areas of tremendous diversity that have undergone rapid change in recent years. Many of the city's best new roasteries are based in East London and a range of artisan coffee venues provide fuel for the artists, students and urbanites who flock here for the weekend markets.

Inner East

* NEW
◊ TOP 30

Allpress Espresso Bar Shoreditch

58 Redchurch Street, E2 7DP

The famous Allpress Redchurch Street café helped catapult a once neglected side road into one of East London's hippest retail streets. The Kiwi roaster's influence extends well beyond the local area, though; with wholesale coffee customers spanning the length and breadth of the country. Following the opening of the company's new Dalston Roastery Café, this original site was refurbished with a smaller, yet still perfectly-formed footprint, ideally positioned for a post-shopping espresso and a spot of people-watching.

+44(0)20 7749 1780
uk.allpressespresso.com
⊖ Shoreditch High Street

Sister locations Dalston

| MON-FRI. | 7:30am - 5:00pm |
| SAT-SUN. | 9:00am - 5:00pm |

First opened 2010
Roaster Allpress Espresso
Machine La Marzocco Linea PB, 3 groups
Grinder Mazzer Kold, Mazzer Super Jolly

Espresso	£2.20
Cappuccino	£2.80
Latte	£2.80
Flat white	£2.80

MAP REF. 118

COFFEE
4.75 / 5

OVERALL
4.25 / 5 ★★★★⯪

The Attendant Shoreditch

74 Great Eastern Street, EC2A 3JL

The original Attendant in Foley Street might seem a hard act to follow, between its excellent quality and its inimitable location. This new one is quite a big place, light and airy, and beautifully decorated with lots of greenery. With the expanded space comes an expansive food offering, baked goods in the morning leading on to brunch or lunch of soup, sandwiches, salads and the like. Attendant's roastery produces beans that make for a rounded, fruity cup, and for a very pleasant Shoreditch sojourn.

+44(0)20 7739 3143
www.the-attendant.com
⊖ Old Street

Sister locations Fitzrovia

MON-FRI.	8:00am - 6:00pm
SAT-SUN.	9:00am - 6:00pm

First opened 2015
Roaster The Attendant
Machine La Marzocco GB5, 2 groups
Grinder Mazzer Kold

Espresso	£2.00
Cappuccino	£2.80
Latte	£2.80
Flat white	£2.80

MAP REF. 119

COFFEE 4.25 / 5	OVERALL 4.00 / 5

Barber & Parlour

64-66 Redchurch Street, E2 7DP

Barber and Parlour is a hybrid space on achingly hip Redchurch Street, catering for the East Londoner's every whim. The visitor will encounter a cinema, hair salon, nail bar, and gentleman's barber before reaching the kitchen on the upper floor. Skilled baristas diligently oversee the coffee preparation. With excellent Origin beans in the hopper, coffee aficionados have their caffeine fix sorted. The only choice that remains: will you be following your espresso with a moustache trim or a Brazilian?

+44(0)20 3376 1777
www.barberandparlour.com
⊖ Shoreditch High Street

MON-SUN. 9:00am - 9:30pm

First opened 2014
Roaster Origin Coffee Roasters and guests
Machine La Marzocco Linea PB, 3 groups
Grinder Nuova Simonelli Mythos,
Mazzer Super Jolly

Espresso	£2.50
Cappuccino	£3.00
Latte	£3.00
Flat white	£3.00

Sister locations Hubbard & Bell

MAP REF. 120

COFFEE 4.25 / 5

OVERALL 4.25 / 5 ★★★★☆

Brooklyn Coffee

139 Commercial Street, E1 6BJ

The slick interior design of Brooklyn Coffee divides opinion. It's all clean lines, sharp corners and plate glass. The effect is multiplied by the monolithic concrete bar. Well-extracted Caravan coffee is made with precision by co-owner Bryan, who originally hails from New York City himself. Complement your flat white with a bar of artisan chocolate crafted by Williamsburg's achingly hip Mast Brothers. The store's interior may be austere, but the North American-style hospitality at Brooklyn Coffee is attentive and friendly.

www.brooklyncoffee.co.uk
⊖ Shoreditch High Street /
Liverpool Street

MON-FRI.	7:00am - 5:00pm
SAT.	8:00am - 5:00pm
SUN.	9:00am - 5:00pm

First opened 2014
Roaster Caravan Coffee Roasters
Machine La Marzocco Linea PB, 2 groups
Grinder Mazzer Robur, Mazzer Kony

Espresso	£2.40
Cappuccino	£2.80
Latte	£3.00
Flat white	£2.80

MAP REF.

COFFEE 4.50 / 5

OVERALL 4.50 / 5 ★★★★✦

Bulldog Edition at Ace Hotel

100 Shoreditch High Street, E1 6JQ

Bulldog Edition is nestled in the Ace Hotel, a hip hotel in ever-fashionable Shoreditch. The coffee bar opens into the lobby, providing ample seating and first-rate people-watching opportunities. Drawing on Square Mile's expertise, Bulldog presents an innovative coffee menu, including filter shots and strong filter-style coffee extracted with the espresso machine at low pressure. The knowledgeable baristas run a smooth service with impeccable attention to detail, setting a new quality benchmark for hotel coffee.

+44(0)20 7613 9800
www.acehotel.com/london
Shoreditch High Street / Old Street

MON-SUN.   6:30am - 6:00pm

First opened 2013
Roaster Square Mile Coffee Roasters
Machine La Marzocco Strada, 3 groups
Grinder La Marzocco Vulcano,
Mahlkönig EK 43

Espresso	£2.00 / £2.20
Cappuccino	£2.60
Latte	£3.00
Flat white	£2.60

MAP REF. **122**

COFFEE 4.75 / 5

OVERALL 4.50 / 5 ★★★★⯪

The Canvas Café

42 Hanbury Street, E1 5JL

There are lots of places to have a coffee around Brick Lane, but Canvas is a standout. This pleasantly shabby-looking place is part of a network of 'Happy Cafés,' aimed at promoting contentment through spiritual, artistic, and intellectual improvement. Don't worry: Canvas is a place for fun, even if you don't want a compassion course or storytelling session. Weekday food is eggs, salads, baked things and sandwiches. Brunch reigns at weekends. Friendly, well trained staff pull tiptop espresso-based coffees using Square Mile beans. Check out the writing on the walls, and add to it.

+44(0)20 7018 1020
www.thecanvascafe.org/cafe
Liverpool Street / Shoreditch High Street

MON.	Closed
TUE-FRI.	9:00am - 9:00pm
SAT-SUN.	10:00am - 8:00pm
WINTER:	
TUE-SUN.	10:00am - 6:00pm

First opened 2014
Roaster Square Mile Coffee Roasters
Machine La Marzocco Linea, 2 groups
Grinder Mazzer

Espresso	£2.20
Cappuccino	£2.70
Latte	£2.70
Flat white	£2.60

MAP REF. 123

COFFEE
4.00 / 5

OVERALL
4.25 / 5 ★★★★⯪

Cream

31 New Inn Yard, EC2A 3EY

Now well established on the East London scene, Cream continue to bring their innovative cooking to their large converted warehouse space. The Dark Arts coffee is very well prepared, but the food deserves a special mention. With a daily changing menu featuring what's market fresh, you can be sure to find something to tempt you. When it comes to brunch, Cream definitely rises to the top.

+44(0)7931 289 260
www.cream-shoreditch.com
Shoreditch High Street

MON–FRI. 8:00am – 4:00pm
SAT–SUN. 10:00am – 5:00pm

First opened 2015
Roaster Dark Arts Coffee
Machine Kees van der Westen Mirage, 2 groups
Grinder Compak K-10 x2, Compak K-3

Espresso £2.00
Cappuccino £2.40
Latte £2.40
Flat white £2.40

MAP REF. 124

COFFEE 4.50 / 5	OVERALL 4.50 / 5

Exmouth Coffee Company

83 Whitechapel High Street, E1 7QX

In a city now peppered with cool Antipodean cafés, Exmouth stands out with its refreshingly eclectic mixture of East End and North African influences. Situated next to Whitechapel Gallery, this lively venue attracts a diverse, arty crowd. Roasted in-house, the coffee is dark and chocolaty. Food is freshly prepared in front of customers, and extraordinarily presented. From flatbread sandwiches to an enticing array of baked goods, Exmouth's offering will keep you coming back for more.

+44(0)20 7377 1010
www.exmouthcoffee.co.uk
⊖ Aldgate East

MON–SUN. 7:00am - 8:00pm

First opened 2012
Roaster Exmouth Coffee Company
Machine La Marzocco Strada, 3 groups
Grinder Mazzer Robur, Mahlkönig EK 43, Mahlkönig Air

Espresso	£2.20
Cappuccino	£2.95
Latte	£2.95
Flat white	£2.95

MAP REF. 125

COFFEE 4.00 / 5		OVERALL 4.25 / 5	★★★★✦

Fix 126

126 Curtain Road, EC2A 3PJ

The second Fix location in the heart of Shoreditch is a hub of creativity and a popular place for local freelancers to meet and collaborate, or simply work alone on laptops or sketchbooks. This is also an excellent spot to stop for a daily caffeine fix, and friendly staff are happy to chat while whipping up a cup of Climpson's espresso or Caravan coffee. A stool at one of the large front windows is the ideal place to sit and watch the comings and goings along vibrant Curtain Road.

+44(0)20 7033 9555
www.fix-coffee.co.uk
⊖ Old Street / Shoreditch High Street

Sister locations Fix

MON–FRI. 7:00am - 7:00pm
SAT–SUN. 8:00am - 7:00pm

First opened 2011
Roaster Climpson & Sons, Caravan Coffee Roasters
Machine La Marzocco GB/5, 3 groups
Grinder Nuova Simonelli Mythos x2, Mazzer Robur E

Espresso	£1.60 / £2.00
Cappuccino	£2.50 / £2.70
Latte	£2.50 / £2.70
Flat white	£2.50

MAP REF. 126

COFFEE 4.25 / 5		OVERALL 4.00 / 5	★★★★☆

Friends of Ours

61 Pitfield Street, N1 6BU

You feel instantly at home in this neighbourhood hangout, even if it's your first visit. Coffee comes from Dark Arts, expertly made on the Victoria Arduino Black Eagle Gravitech. But coffee alone doesn't sum up this venue's appeal. Regulars abound, the owners 'wanted this to be a place where we would remember names and orders.' During the week, most custom is takeaway; at weekends it swings closer to 90 per cent eating-in for the coffee and fine brunch fare.

+44(0)7545 939 751
www.friendsofourscafe.com
⊖ Old Street

MON–FRI.	8:00am – 5:00am
SAT.	9:00am – 5:00pm
SUN.	10:00am – 5:00pm

First opened 2015
Roaster Dark Arts Coffee
Machine Victoria Arduino Black Eagle Gravitech, 2 groups
Grinder Mahlkönig EK 43, Nuova Simonelli Mythos One

Espresso	£2.20
Cappuccino	£2.80
Latte	£2.80
Flat white	£2.70

MAP REF. 127

COFFEE 4.50 / 5

OVERALL 4.25 / 5 ★★★★½

Holy Shot Coffee

155 Bethnal Green Road, E2 7DG

Michael Kim came into coffee via the personal route. He worked in finance, but felt more passionate about the black stuff than the green stuff. After travelling and researching extensively, he opened this new Bethnal Green space. It's nice to look at and a pleasure to sit in, with one big table and potted plants in abundance. Caravan's espresso blend is racy stuff, best displayed in combination with milk, and it's expertly crafted here. Have a little something baked. And do consider taking home a bar of their mega-popular homemade coffee soap.

www.holyshotcoffee.com
⊖ Shoreditch High Street

MON-FRI.	7:00am - 7:00pm
SAT.	8:00am - 7:00pm
SUN.	8:00am - 6:00pm

First opened 2016
Roaster Caravan Coffee Roasters
Machine La Marzocco Linea PB, 2 groups
Grinder Mazzer Kony

Espresso	£2.00
Cappuccino	£2.50
Latte	£2.50
Flat white	£2.50

MAP REF. **128**

COFFEE 4.00 / 5   OVERALL 4.00 / 5   ★★★★☆

Jonestown

215 Bethnal Green Road, E2 6AB

Serial coffee entrepreneur Adrian Jones opened Jonestown in 2015, on a corner site with a bit of pavement seating and a very great deal of bright, almost Caribbean colouring in the decorative scheme. Or perhaps it's meant to evoke Papua New Guinea, which is where all their coffee comes from (though they won't say who roasted it). Whatever the source, it makes this patch of Bethnal Green look just great.

And the professionalism of the café operation reflects Jones' 20 years in the industry. Everything runs smoothly, with a small team turning out quality brews and simple food – and always with a smile. Espresso from the La Marzocco, a double shot, is sweet enough to need no

sugar. Latte art is notably accomplished. The café's corner site offers a good view of Bethnal Green Road. While pavement tables are a treat in fine weather, the indoor seating option of choice is the sofa, so comfortable you'll need coffee just to keep from falling asleep.

Even as Bethnal Green becomes one of London's coffee hotspots, this is a local star. Note: those who remember the 1970s need not worry: there's no connection between this Jonestown and the one in Guyana.

MAP REF.

COFFEE 4.25 / 5	OVERALL 4.50 / 5

Inner East

MON–SAT.	7:00am – 7:00pm
SUN.	8:00am – 7:00pm

First opened 2015
Machine La Marzocco Linea AV, 3 groups
Grinder Mazzer Kold, Mahlkönig EK 43

Espresso	£1.70
Cappuccino	£2.50
Latte	£2.50
Flat white	£2.50

+44(0)20 7739 7476
www.jonestown.co.uk
 Bethnal Green

Kahaila

135 Brick Lane, E1 6SB

Kahaila began life in 2012 as a café and local gathering place for events. Since then it has become very popular, the large room at the back crowded with groups, couples, and Brick Lane creatives tap-tapping on their devices. Coffee is a big part of the draw: very well made using beans from Climpson, and with three different grinders showing their attention to detail. The food offering is basic, but the big room is a very pleasant place to eat it. Even in an area that's pretty rich with coffee, Kahaila is a hot spot.

+44(0)20 7998 1388
www.kahaila.com
🚇 Liverpool Street

MON.	9:30am – 7:00pm
TUE-FRI.	8:30am – 7:00pm
SAT.	9:30am – 7:00pm
SUN.	9:30am – 5:30pm

First opened 2012
Roaster Climpson & Sons
Machine La Marzocco GB5, 2 groups
Grinder Mazzer Robur, Mazzer Major, Mahlkönig EK 43

Espresso	£2.20
Cappuccino	£2.80
Latte	£2.80
Flat white	£2.80

MAP REF. **130**

COFFEE 4.00 / 5	OVERALL 4.00 / 5
🫘🫘🫘🫘🫘	★★★★☆

Lantana Shoreditch

1 Oliver's Yard, 55 City Road, EC1Y 1HQ

This branch of Lantana (previously named Salvation Jane) has helped transform East London's once arid coffee landscape into a blossoming caffeine community. A takeout bar serves those in a rush, and the large midcentury-inspired casual dining room is a fashionable spot for brunch. Lantana's formidable brunch menu and potent Alchemy coffee (a unique blend available at Lantana only) are more than a match for even the most grievous Shoreditch hangover.

+44(0)20 7253 5273
www.lantanacafe.co.uk
⊖ Old Street

Sister locations Fitzrovia / Camden

MON-FRI. 7:30am - 10:00pm
SAT-SUN. 9:00am - 5:00pm

First opened 2012
Roaster Alchemy bespoke blend and guests
Machine La Marzocco FB/80, 3 groups
Grinder Mazzer Robur E x2

Espresso	£2.20
Cappuccino	£2.80 / £3.00
Latte	£2.80 / £3.00
Flat white	£2.80 / £3.00

MAP REF.

COFFEE 4.50 / 5	OVERALL 4.50 / 5
●●●●◗	★★★★⯪

143

Lmnh Kitchen

101 Back Church Lane, E1 8LU

You don't need to be a two-wheel-wonder to have fun at Look Mum No Hands! in Old Street, consuming great coffee and good food while surrounded by a cross-section of the local Shoreditch scene. At the group's second venue, the motto might be 'Don't say Look Mum No Hands'! This recent addition to the Whitechapel coffee scene is indeed a creation of the Shoreditch café, but there's hardly a bike in sight. And certainly no repairs taking place. So they've rebranded acronymically.

Lmnh occupies a gorgeous ground-floor space in The Loom, a Victorian wool warehouse turned creative complex. When you're sitting here you can see through a glass partition into the lobby, but you never feel that you're in an architectural afterthought. Through clever and sensitive design, Lmnh has made this into a place that feels - and in fact is - a proper café/restaurant. Food can be anything from cakes or cheese plates to sharing platters and full meals, with dinner service two nights a week. Coffee comes from Square Mile by way of a cosseted Kees van der Westen, and it's made with consummate skill. Service is charming, and the drinks list is serious (check out the London-brewed beer selection). Weekend brunch after a walk around Whitechapel? Yes please, mum!

MAP REF.

| COFFEE 4.50 / 5 | OVERALL 4.50 / 5 ★★★★⯪ |

Inner East

MON–WED.	7:30am – 5:00pm
THU–FRI.	7:30am – 11:00pm
SAT–SUN.	8:00am – 4:00pm

Sister locations Look Mum No Hands!

First opened 2016
Roaster Square Mile Coffee Roasters
and guests
Machine Kees van der Westen, 3 groups
Grinder Nuova Simonelli Mythos One, Anfim

Espresso	£2.20
Cappuccino	£2.90
Latte	£2.90
Flat white	£2.90

www.lookmumnohands.com
⊖ Aldgate East

Lyle's

Tea Building, 56 Shoreditch High Street, E1 6JJ

With a few exceptions, restaurants are guilty of some grievous crimes against coffee. At Lyle's you can eat very handsomely (seasonal, unfussy fare) and conclude your meal with a jaw-dropping espresso. If you're in the mood for a coffee and nothing more, that's fine too. The bar is an all-day affair offering exceptional beans from the likes of Sweden's Koppi and Belleville in Paris. At Lyle's, coffee is treated with the same respect as food and wine, challenging entrenched perceptions of how restaurants think about coffee.

+44(0)20 3011 5911
www.lyleslondon.com
⊖ Shoreditch High Street

MON–FRI.	8:00am – 11:00pm
SAT.	12:00pm – 11:00pm
SUN.	Closed

First opened 2014
Roaster Belleville, Roundhill, La Cabra, James Gourmet, Koppi, Clifton
Machine Nuova Simonelli Aurelia II T3, 2 groups
Grinder Mahlkönig EK 43

Espresso	£2.00
Cappuccino	£2.50
Latte	£2.70
Flat white	£2.50

MAP REF. **133**

COFFEE
4.50 / 5

OVERALL
4.25 / 5 ★★★★⯪

Modern Society

33 Redchurch Street, E2 7DJ

Modern Society is a lovely little café. Not surprising, since it's located in a store that sells high-end clothing, accessories and housewares. But it maximises the wow factor with particularly gorgeous floor tiles and chandeliers. Perch at the bar or grab the single table and sit right in the window to watch the hip pageantry of Redchurch Street float by. The coffee operation has been put in place with help from Embassy East, around the corner, and it's ultra-professional. Note the filtered options supplementing the espresso-based list. And note the reasonable prices, too.

themodernsociety.com/modern-society-cafe/
Shoreditch High Street

MON-FRI.	10:00am - 7:00pm
SAT-SUN.	11:00am - 5:00pm

First opened 2015
Roaster Assembly
Machine Modbar, 2 groups
Grinder Nuova Simonelli Mythos One

Espresso	£2.00
Cappuccino	£2.20
Latte	£2.20
Flat white	£2.20

COFFEE 4.25 / 5   **OVERALL** 4.25 / 5 ★★★★⯪

Nkora

21 Hackney Road, E2 7NX

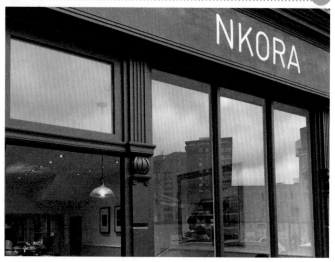

Nkora hums with the happy feeling you get from an attractive room, skilled, friendly staff, and a real commitment to neighbourhood. The food offer is low-key; sandwiches and baked goods. Coffee encompasses Aeropress and V60 in addition to the espresso-based drinks (made to a high standard by ultra-friendly baristas). The neighbourhood touches come in the form of a downstairs work space with a big table, mum-and-baby groups on Wednesdays, and a positively ecstatic policy on Man's Best Friend: 'We love dogs!'

nkora.co.uk
⊖ Shoreditch High Street

MON-FRI. 7:30am - 5:00pm
SAT-SUN. 9:00am - 6:00pm

First opened 2015
Roaster Union Coffee Roasters
Machine La Marzocco Linea PB, 2 groups
Grinder Mahlkönig EK 43

Espresso	£2.20
Cappuccino	£2.70
Latte	£2.70
Flat white	£2.70

MAP REF. 135

COFFEE
4.25 / 5

OVERALL
4.25 / 5 ★★★★⯪

Nude Espresso Hanbury Street

26 Hanbury Street, E1 6QR

Located close to the bustling Spitalfields and Brick Lane markets, Nude Espresso is one of London's busiest weekend destinations for coffee lovers. Nude offers much more than just a pitstop for weekend shoppers, with its famous 'East' espresso blend and hearty brunch options making it well worth braving the mobs any day of the week. The Nude Roastery itself is just across the road, for anyone who is interested in seeing live coffee roasting in progress.

+44(0)7712 899 335
www.nudeespresso.com
Shoreditch High Street / Liverpool Street

Sister locations The Roastery (Hanbury St) / Bell Lane / Spitalfields Market

MON-FRI.	7:00am – 6:00pm
SAT-SUN.	9:30am – 5:00pm

First opened 2008
Roaster Nude Coffee Roasters
Machine La Marzocco Linea PB, 3 groups
Grinder Nuova Simonelli Mythos

Espresso	£2.40
Cappuccino	£3.00
Latte	£3.00
Flat white	£3.00

MAP REF. **136**

COFFEE 4.75 / 5

OVERALL 4.50 / 5 ★★★★⯪

Origin Coffee Roasters Charlotte Road

65 Charlotte Road, EC2A 3PE

Photo: Juliet Murphy

Origin buys green beans through direct trade with producers and roasts them in Cornwall, where the company is based. This small London outpost does the beans proud, both in espresso and in a surprisingly popular brew bar (around 20 per cent of their trade is non-espresso-based). The ground-floor café is soothingly attractive, and there's a full training centre downstairs where they offer SCAE courses covering barista skills at every level. Food is simple, service friendly and attentive. Now a key venue within the sophisticated Shoreditch coffee scene.

+44(0)1326 574 337
www.origincoffee.co.uk
Old Street

MON–FRI.	7:30am – 6:00pm
SAT.	10:00am – 6:00pm
SUN	11:00am – 5:00pm

First opened 2014
Roaster Origin Coffee Roasters
Machine La Marzocco Strada, 3 groups
Grinder Nuova Simonelli Mythos One, Mahlkönig EK 43

Espresso	£2.50
Cappuccino	£3.00
Latte	£3.00
Flat white	£3.00

MAP REF. **137**

COFFEE 4.50 / 5

OVERALL 4.50 / 5 ★★★★✬

Ozone Coffee Roasters

11 Leonard Street, EC2A 4AQ

TOP
35

This huge dual-level roastery, café and bar represents a stunning feature of London's coffee scene. A central island on the first floor contains an open kitchen, around which are arrayed bar stools where customers can sip a brew and watch their food being prepared. Further seating is provided downstairs, in view of the magnificent Probat roaster. Ozone's decor is a combination of Victorian industrial, Kiwi kitsch, and South American barrio, resulting in a contemporary yet welcoming atmosphere that exudes an overarching passion for coffee.

+44(0)20 7490 1039
www.ozonecoffee.co.uk
⊖ Old Street

MON-FRI.	7:30am - 9:00pm
SAT-SUN.	9:00am - 5:00pm

First opened 2012
Roaster Ozone Coffee Roasters
Machine La Marzocco Strada, 3 groups
Grinder Mahlkönig EK 43, Nuova Simonelli Mythos One, Mazzer Kold

Espresso	£2.40
Cappuccino	£3.00
Latte	£3.00
Flat white	£3.00

MAP REF.

COFFEE
5 / 5

OVERALL
5 / 5

Shoreditch Grind

213 Old Street, EC1V 9NR

With its retro cinema signage, circular interior, and prime location right on the Old Street 'Silicon Roundabout', Shoreditch Grind is coffee theatre at its finest. Coffee lovers can sit on bar stools and look out at one of the city's busiest transport hubs while feeling insulated from the rat race with a cup of delicious custom-blended coffee in hand. As the Shoreditch night draws in, the café turns into a hip bar serving beers, wines, and cocktails. The venue also has a recording studio which is available for musicians to hire.

+44(0)20 7490 7490
www.shoreditchgrind.com
Old Street (Exit 8)

Sister locations Clerkenwell / Covent Garden / Holborn / London Grind / Royal Exchange / Soho

MON–THU.	7:00am – 11:00pm
FRI.	7:00am – 1:00am
SAT.	8:00am – 1:00am
SUN.	9:00am – 7:00pm

First opened 2011
Roaster The Grind House Espresso
Machine La Marzocco Linea PB, 2 groups x2
Grinder Nuova Simonelli Mythos One x3, Mahlkönig Tanzania

Espresso	£2.20
Cappuccino	£2.90 / £3.20
Latte	£2.90 / £3.20
Flat white	£2.80

MAP REF. **139**

COFFEE 4.50 / 5

OVERALL 4.50 / 5 ★★★★⯪

Trade

47 Commercial Street, E1 6BD

Trade is a neatly-pulled-together outfit among the textile wholesalers of Spitalfields, dealing in stout sandwiches and a no-nonsense approach to coffee making. The painted brick walls and industrial fittings may be rather hackneyed, but the interior is well-planned, spacious, and wholly redeemed by a sun-splashed terrace. Prepare to reckon with bold brunch and lunch options including formidable lobster rolls and reuben sandwiches. Boasting walloping fare and well-made coffee, Trade is a juicy morsel on an otherwise unappetising strip of Commercial Street.

+44(0)20 3490 1880
www.trade-made.co.uk
⊖ Aldgate East

| MON-FRI. | 7:30am – 5:00pm |
| SAT-SUN. | 9:00am – 5:00pm |

First opened 2014
Roaster Origin Coffee Roasters and guests
Machine Orchestrale Etnica, 2 groups
Grinder Nuova Simonelli Mythos One

Espresso	£1.90
Cappuccino	£2.50
Latte	£2.50
Flat white	£2.50

MAP REF. 140

COFFEE 4.25 / 5 🫘🫘🫘🫘🫘

OVERALL 4.25 / 5 ★★★★⯪

Vagabond at Trade Union

Building 3, Thomas More Square, E1W 1YZ

Finding this branch of Vagabond can be tricky the first time, but you'll be happy to have made the effort. This is a really good place in a really unusual space, sharing the ground floor of an office block with a bar, a restaurant, and a - wait for it - barber shop. Talk about one-stop shopping. And not only is the space unusual, it's a pleasure to behold. Barista skills are formidable here, with great latte art. There's a good selection of alternative brew methods, and tasty sandwiches and baked items.

www.vagabond.london
⊖ Tower Hill

Sister locations Vagabond N7 / Vagabond N4 / Vagabond E1 / Charlotte Street

MON-FRI.	8:00am - 3:30pm
SAT.	9:00am - 3:00pm
SUN.	Closed

First opened 2016
Roaster Vagabond Coffee Roasters
Machine Conti Monte Carlo, 3 groups
Grinder Compak E8

Espresso	£2.00
Cappuccino	£2.60
Latte	£2.60
Flat white	£2.60

MAP REF.

| COFFEE 4.50 / 5 | | OVERALL 4.25 / 5 | |

White Mulberries

D3 Ivory House, St Katharine Docks, E1W 1AT

Like its namesake, White Mulberries is a sweet find: a rare combination of beautiful setting and great coffee. Located in St Katharine Docks - London's little-known marina - it offers visitors an enviable view of the swan-like sailboats. The café really comes into its own in fine weather when outdoor seating is provided overlooking the water. Customers are treated to a rotating range of beans from top UK and international microroasters. Accompany your coffee with an award-winning 'super moist' brownie and sail away to heaven.

www.whitemulberries.com
◉ Tower Hill / Tower Gateway DLR

MON-FRI.	7:30am - 5:00pm
SAT.	8:00am - 6:00pm
SUN.	8:30am - 6:00pm

First opened 2012
Roaster Allpress Espresso and guest roasters
Machine La Marzocco FB/80, 2 groups
Grinder Nuovo Simonelli Mythos, Mazzer Major, Mazzer Super Jolly

Espresso	£2.00 / £2.50
Cappuccino	£3.00 / £3.50
Latte	£3.00 / £3.50
Flat white	£3.00 / £3.50

MAP REF. **142**

JOIN THE PLANT-BASED REVOLUTION

East London has successfully shaken off its label as a rough outer region to emerge as London's booming artistic neighbourhood. A wonderful combination of cultures and a thriving creative scene have helped put the area back on the map, and provide a fertile environment for London's coffee pioneers.

East

46b Espresso Hut

46b Brooksby's Walk, E9 6DA

Locals should seriously consider altering their morning commute expressly to visit 46b. Visitors from elsewhere will discover some of the best coffee served in Hackney in this unassuming, yet enchanting café. The zesty Red Brick blend pulled through the Seattle-made Synesso Cyncra is worth travelling for. Scrupulously selected suppliers include Northiam Dairy, E5 Bakehouse, and London Borough of Jam. 46b is Hackney's quietly brilliant venue.

+44(0)7702 063 172
⊖ Homerton

MON-FRI.	7:30am – 6:00pm
SAT.	9:00am – 6:00pm
SUN.	9:30am – 5:00pm

First opened 2012
Roaster Square Mile Coffee Roasters
Machine Synesso Cyncra, 2 groups
Grinder Anfim Super Caimano, Mazzer Super Jolly

Espresso	£2.00
Cappuccino	£2.50
Latte	£2.50
Flat white	£2.50

MAP REF. 143

COFFEE 4.50 / 5   **OVERALL** 4.25 / 5 ★★★★✦

56 St James

56 St James Street, E17 7PE

56 St James is a true neighbourhood coffee shop. There's something for everyone here: delicious coffee, the large communal table, a gigantic chalkboard for children, and cakes handmade by none other than the owner's mum. This café also has a penchant for pineapples: pineapple themed art cheerfully graces the walls and visitors are greeted by an enormous pineapple donning the exterior brickwork. In past centuries, this exotic fruit was a symbol of prosperity. 56 St James is a sure sign that Walthamstow's fortunes are on the up.

+44(0)7792 328 479
⇌ St James Street

MON-TUE.	Closed
WED-THU.	9:00am – 6:00pm
FRI.	9:00am – 4:30pm | 6:00pm – 11:00pm
SAT-SUN.	10:00am – 6:00pm

First opened 2014
Roaster Nude Espresso
Machine La Marzocco Linea, 2 groups
Grinder Compak K-10, Compak K-3

Espresso	£2.00
Cappuccino	£2.50
Latte	£2.50
Flat white	£2.50

MAP REF. 144

COFFEE 4.00 / 5   **OVERALL** 4.00 / 5 ★★★★☆

Allpress Espresso Roastery & Café

Dalston 55 Dalston Lane, E8 2NG

Allpress is a powerful outfit, and very popular locally. This impressive Allpress roastery occupies a large and airy space on both floors of a converted joiner's factory. Expect distinct crowds: City types, mums and even students on weekday mornings, with a more mixed clientele later in the day and at weekends. Espresso-based drinks are made flawlessly, as you'd expect from Allpress, but pour-over is executed with care. As is everything from the kitchen. Note that there is no WiFi because the owners 'want to give people a place where they can get away from work and socialise.'

+44(0)20 7749 1780
uk.allpressespresso.com
⊖ Dalston Junction

Sister locations Shoreditch

MON.	7:30am – 3:00pm
	(take-away only)
TUE-FRI.	7:30am – 4:00pm
SAT-SUN.	9:00am – 4:00pm

First opened 2015
Roaster Allpress Espresso
Machine La Marzocco Linea PB, 3 groups
Grinder Mazzer Kold, Mazzer Super Jolly

Espresso	£2.20
Cappuccino	£2.80
Latte	£2.80
Flat white	£2.80

MAP REF. 145

| COFFEE 4.50 / 5 | OVERALL 5 / 5 ★★★★★ |

163

Brunswick East

Unit 3D Stamford Works, Gillett Street, N16 8JH

Nestled in the midst of a humming complex of offices and studios (as well as the skate-park in Gillett Square), Brunswick East is a small, ultra-friendly operation owned by two Australian sisters. They set out with three main aims. One: recreate Oz-style brunch ('our favourite meal'). Two: provide a central meeting place for the local workers who, they felt, usually operate in isolation. Three: make great coffee. They set about the task with lively spins on the Aussie breakfast and lunch staple dishes, and with Alchemy coffee expertly made. Mission accomplished.

+44(0)7570 119 708
www.brunswickeast.london
Dalston Kingsland

MON-FRI.	8:00am - 6:00pm
SAT.	9:00am - 5:00pm
SUN.	10:00am - 5:00pm

First opened 2015
Roaster Alchemy Coffee Roasters
Machine La Marzocco Linea, 2 groups
Grinder Mazzer Kony E, Mahlkönig EK 43

Espresso	£2.20
Cappuccino	£2.80
Latte	£2.80
Flat white	£2.80

MAP REF. 146

COFFEE 4.25 / 5   **OVERALL** 4.00 / 5 ★★★★☆

Bühler and Co

8 Chingford Road, E17 4PJ

Sisters Meg and Rosie Bühler created their café with the view that it needed to have 'good coffee, good food, good service, and a good environment.' They're four for four. This attractive Walthamstow local does everything right, from the warm smiles through unusually ambitious and imaginative food to beautifully brewed coffee from Climpson beans. This is a real standout in an area that's not overly supplied with good coffee, and the locals have taken it to their hearts. Check out the garden - blankets provided for when the weather's cold.

+44(0)20 8527 3652
www.buhlerandco.com
⊖ Walthamstow Central

MON.	Closed
TUE-FRI.	8:00am - 5:00pm
SAT-SUN.	9:00am - 5:00pm

First opened 2016
Roaster Climpson & Sons
Machine La Marzocco Linea, 2 groups
Grinder Mazzer Major, Mahlkönig Tanzania

Espresso	£2.20
Cappuccino	£2.50
Latte	£2.50
Flat white	£2.50

MAP REF. **147**

Climpson & Sons

67 Broadway Market, E8 4PH

Climpson is one of London's star roasters, and its flagship café has been a star in Broadway Market since 2005. Unless you savour the hustle and bustle (and queues) on market-day weekends, the week is the best time to come. Your brew will be served in ceramic, not paper, and you'll be able to enjoy it along with locals who love to drink and laugh. Milky drinks are made with exceptional care and skill, and the breakfast and lunch menu features ingredients bought from local suppliers.

www.climpsonandsons.com

⊖ Haggerston / ⇌ Cambridge Heath Rail

Sister locations Broadway Market Stall (Sat only) / Climpson's Arch Roastery & Coffee Bar

MON-FRI.	7:30am - 5:00pm
SAT.	8:30am - 5:00pm
SUN.	9:00am - 5:00pm

First opened 2005
Roaster Climpson & Sons
Machine La Marzocco PB , 3 groups, La Marzocco AV, 3 groups
Grinder Nuova Simonelli Mythos One, Mahlkönig EK 43

Espresso	£2.00
Cappuccino	£2.60
Latte	£2.60
Flat white	£2.60

MAP REF. **148**

COFFEE 4.50 / 5

OVERALL 4.25 / 5 ★★★★⯨

Coffee7

10 Sebert Road, E7 0NQ

If you could imagine the perfect neighbourhood coffee shop, you might come up with something that looked like Coffee7. It looks and feels cool but casual, with a succession of small rooms leading to the pretty back garden. (There's even a sunken 'reading room', with bookcases and comfortable seating.) Upstairs there's a room used for yoga, meetings, and serious evening restaurant popups. The assertive Allpress espresso blend forms the basis for all the coffee drinks, and the café menu is simple and fairly priced. Small wonder that they know nearly all their customers by name.

www.coffee7.co.uk

🚆 Forest Gate Rail

MON-TUE.	8:00am – 5:00pm
WED-FRI.	8:00am – 11:00pm
SAT.	9:00am – 11:00pm
SUN.	10:00am – 4:00pm

First opened 2012
Roaster Allpress Espresso
Machine La Marzocco Linea, 2 groups
Grinder Mazzer Major

Espresso	£1.50
Cappuccino	£2.50
Latte	£2.50
Flat white	£2.50

MAP REF. **149**

 COFFEE 4.00 / 5   **OVERALL** 4.25 / 5 ★★★★

167

The Common E2

53 Old Bethnal Green Road, E2 6QA

The Common grew out of the owner's architectural studio, which he still runs on the premises. It was designed to be an 'open work space' for creative people from the local area and beyond, and the main communal table is likely to be crowded with people working on laptops. But there's a nice buzz anyway, coming from friends with friends, mothers with children, and sometimes from the workers themselves, who have meetings and share ideas. Eavesdropping is a serious temptation.

And the buzz comes also from the friendly, chatty, helpful staff. Food and drink are excellent, with eggs and good toasted sandwiches prominent (at extremely reasonable prices), and superbly made brews using beans from The Roasting Shed in Clapton.

At the time of writing, Common E2 was greatly expanding its kitchen facilities in the basement and hiring a chef with the promise of many more cooked dishes. The Common is already firmly committed to community, featuring work by local artists in addition to photos and drawings from the owner's architectural practice. Its expanded food offer should put the place even more firmly on the Bethnal Green map.

MAP REF. 150

COFFEE 4.25 / 5	OVERALL 4.50 / 5

MON-FRI.	8:30am - 5:30pm
SAT-SUN.	9:30am - 5:30pm

First opened 2015
Roaster The Roasting Shed and guests
Machine La Marzocco Linea PB, 2 groups
Grinder Mazzer Super Jolly

Espresso	£2.00
Cappuccino	£2.80
Latte	£2.80
Flat white	£2.40

thecommone2.com
⊖ Bethnal Green

Corner Kitchen

58a Woodgrange Road, E7 0QH

Corner Kitchen is a bit of sunshine on traffic-heavy Woodgrange Road. The owners have aimed to make this a community centre as well as a café and restaurant, and you can come here for events including children's play activities in the basement and wine tastings. Or you can just eat and drink. Doppio's espresso blend is a high roast best suited to milky treatment, and it's made well. The restaurant features pizzas and many other baked goods made on the premises, and the wine list is heavy on natural wine.

+44(0)20 8555 8068
www.cornerkitchen.london
⇌ Forest Gate Rail

MON–THU.	9:00am – 10:00pm
FRI–SAT.	9:00am – 10:30pm
SUN.	9:00am – 9:00pm

First opened 2016
Roaster Doppio Coffee
Machine La Marzocco Linea, 2 groups
Grinder Mazzer Super Jolly

Espresso	£1.50
Cappuccino	£2.50
Latte	£2.50
Flat white	£2.50

MAP REF. **151**

COFFEE 4.00 / 5

OVERALL 4.00 / 5 ★★★★☆

Craving Coffee

Unit 3, Gaunson House, Markfield Road, N15 4QQ

Craving Coffee resides in a converted industrial unit shared with The Mill Co. Project studio space. Co-owner Matt Ho formerly roasted with Climpson & Sons, and his experience clearly shines through in the superb coffee service. The kitchen turns out thoughtfully-prepared dishes using seasonal ingredients from local suppliers. This large, versatile space opens weekly for Tottenham Social, where some of London's best street food traders take over the kitchen.

+44(0)20 8808 3178
www.cravingcoffee.co.uk
Seven Sisters / Tottenham Hale

MON-WED.	10:00am – 5:00pm
THU-SAT.	10:00am – 11:00pm
SUN.	10:00am – 5:00pm

First opened 2014
Roaster Climpson & Sons
Machine Synesso Hydra, 2 groups
Grinder Nuova Simonelli Mythos One

Espresso	£2.00
Cappuccino	£2.50
Latte	£2.50
Flat white	£2.50

MAP REF. 152

| COFFEE 4.50 / 5 | | OVERALL 4.25 / 5 | ★★★★⯪ |

Dandy

9-15 Helmsley Place, E8 3SB

Dandy is an exceptionally nice-looking venue, with a skylight running the full length of the room and pale wood in abundance. The exclusive focus on Square Mile means that they know how to get the best out of the blend, while an interesting selection of 'low-intervention' wines features most prominently among the other drinks, making dinner an intriguing proposition. The menu highlights eggs in some novel guises, as well as the usual breakfast suspects. Quick visits for a takeaway coffee are allowed, of course, but the owners prefer to 'engage with people, not ram them through.'

+44(0)20 7923 7877
www.dandycafe.co.uk
London Fields

MON-TUE.	Closed
WED-FRI.	4:00pm – 11:00pm
SAT.	10:00am – 11:00pm
SUN.	10:00am – 6:00pm

First opened 2015
Roaster Square Mile Coffee Roasters
Machine La Marzocco Linea PB, 2 groups
Grinder Mahlkönig EK 43

Espresso	£2.20
Cappuccino	£2.60
Latte	£2.60
Flat white	£2.60

MAP REF. 153

| COFFEE 4.00 / 5 | | OVERALL 4.00 / 5 | ★★★★☆ |

Embassy East

285 Hoxton Street, N1 5JX

Behind the plain exterior and nondescript street address, Embassy East is a café with real soul. Opened on a modest budget, the visitor soon senses the love and ingenuity invested by the founding friends, Chris Coleman and Tommy Studholme (formerly of Flat White). It's the small things that make this Hoxton coffee bar special, like the cleverly modified coffee grinder and quirky pickle jar light fittings. The open kitchen offers carefully prepared breakfast and lunch made fresh with artisanal ingredients.

+44(0)20 7739 8340
www.embassyeast.co.uk
⊖ Hoxton

| MON-FRI. | 9:00am - 5:00pm |
| SAT-SUN. | 10:00am - 5:00pm |

First opened 2013
Roaster Assembly
Machine La Marzocco Linea, 3 groups
Grinder Anfim, Mahlkönig Columbia

Espresso £2.00
Cappuccino £2.20 / £2.50 / £2.70

MAP REF. 154

| COFFEE 4.50 / 5 |  | OVERALL 4.25 / 5 | ★ ★ ★ ★ ✦ |

Esters

55 Kynaston Road, N16 0EB

Stoke Newington residents are fortunate to have such a brilliant little neighbourhood coffee shop on their doorstep. Owners Nia and Jack have created a sanctum where everyone is welcome, from coffee geeks to mums. The food is outstanding and the geeks will be delighted to sample two different filter coffees in addition to espresso-based drinks.

+44(0)20 7254 0253
www.estersn16.com
⇌ Rectory Road Rail /
Stoke Newington Rail

MON.	Closed
TUE-FRI.	8:00am - 4:00pm
SAT.	9:00am - 4:00pm
SUN.	10:00am - 4:00pm

First opened 2013
Roaster Has Bean and guests
Machine La Marzocco Linea, 2 groups
Grinder Nuova Simonelli Mythos One, Mahlkönig EK 43

Espresso £2.20
Cappuccino £2.60
Latte £2.80
Flat white £2.60

MAP REF. 155

| COFFEE 4.25 / 5 |  | OVERALL 4.25 / 5 | ★ ★ ★ ★ ✦ |

Foxcroft & Ginger Whitechapel

69-79 Mile End Road, E1 4TT

Whitechapel's tech startup scene is surging. Creative companies are pouring in, and so are the trendy flat whites. Foxcroft & Ginger's dramatic East End destination fronts an outpost of Central Working, a space for entrepreneurs to grow their businesses. But this café provides much more than just caffeine for coders. Expect a mighty brunch and lunch service with steaming plates of pulled pork and F&G's renowned sourdough pizza. Stick around and join the late-night hackers for a glass of Camden Pale Ale while you hustle for your next killer app idea.

www.foxcroftandginger.co.uk
⊖ Whitechapel / Stepney Green

MON-FRI.	8:00am - 10:00pm
SAT-SUN.	9:00am - 10:00pm

First opened 2014
Roaster The Roasting Party
Machine La Marzocco Linea, 3 groups
Grinder Mazzer Robur, Anfim

Espresso	£2.20
Cappuccino	£2.70
Latte	£2.50 / £2.80
Flat white	£2.70

MAP REF. 156

 COFFEE 4.25 / 5

 OVERALL 4.50 / 5 ★★★★✦

173

The Grand Howl

214a Well Street, E9 6QT

NEW

Two things set Grand Howl apart from most neighbourhood coffee spots. One is the Diedrich roaster at the back which produces all their beans. The other is the all-vegetarian (and mostly vegan) food menu, varied and enticing even for those who eat meat. A lot of business is for takeaway but Howl is an extremely pleasant place to work, talk, or watch the world go by. They keep two espresso selections, one designed for drinking with milk. And that's how the house roasting style shows best. East London is lucky to have this place.

+44(0)20 3659 9631

⊖ Whitechapel / Stepney Green

MON-FRI. 8:30am – 4:30pm
SAT-SUN. 9:00am – 4:00pm

First opened 2016
Roaster Howl
Machine La Marzocco Linea PB, 2 groups
Grinder Nuova Simonelli Mythos One, Mahlkönig EK 43

Espresso	£2.00
Cappuccino	£2.80
Latte	£2.80
Flat white	£2.60

MAP REF. 157

COFFEE 4.25 / 5

OVERALL 4.25 / 5 ★★★★½

Hand Café

20 Victory Parade, E20 1FS

NEW

The vast East Village development in Stratford is lucky to have this coolly laid-back café in its midst, an indie alternative to the chains in nearby Westfield Stratford. A second project from the owner of 46b Espresso Hut in Hackney, Hand has the same Greek-accented menu with an abundance of herbs giving a lift to standard dishes. Square Mile's espresso blend is expertly handled in the Synesso and huge windows bring in plenty of light. There are Greek sweets and other goodies to take home alongside bags of beans, and service couldn't be friendlier.

⊖ Stratford

Sister locations 46b Espresso Hut, Hackney

MON.	8:00am – 6:00pm
TUE.	Closed
WED–FRI.	8:00am – 6:00pm
SAT–SUN.	9:00am – 6:00pm

First opened 2016
Roaster Square Mile Coffee Roasters
Machine Synesso Cyncra, 2 groups
Grinder Nuova Simonelli Mythos One

Espresso	£2.00
Cappuccino	£2.60
Latte	£2.60
Flat white	£2.60

MAP REF. 158

COFFEE
4.25 / 5

OVERALL
4.25 / 5

The Hive Wellbeing

286-290 Cambridge Heath Road, E2 9DA

The word chilled doesn't begin to describe the vibe at this lovely venue, a coffee bar, juice bar, wine bar and restaurant all rolled into one. The Hive Wellbeing comes from the team behind the former G&T. The accent is on healthy, from the all-vegetarian menu to the freshly squeezed fruit juices. But the coffee seems to be what most people come for, and with good reason: The Square Mile blend is crafted perfectly.

+44(0)20 8981 9245
www.thehivewellbeing.com
Bethnal Green /
Cambridge Heath Rail

MON-FRI.	8:00am – 10:00pm
SAT.	9:00am – 10:00pm
SUN.	10:00am – 6:30pm

First opened 2015
Roaster Square Mile Coffee Roasters, Workshop Coffee
Machine La Marzocco FB/80, 2 groups
Grinder Mazzer Kony, Mahlkönig EK 43

Espresso	£2.20
Cappuccino	£2.60
Latte	£2.60
Flat white	£2.60

MAP REF. 159

COFFEE 4.00 / 5
OVERALL 4.25 / 5 ★★★★½

Lanark Coffee

262 Hackney Road, E2 7SJ

Lanark is a little slip of a coffee bar named after Alasdair Gray's dystopian novel. You can rely on owner, Greg Boyce, to fix you a superb brew with an assortment of beans from top microroasters, as well as a range of teas. Coffee geeks will gravitate towards the Victoria Arduino Athena, a mythological lever-operated espresso machine with beautiful hammered metalwork and exquisite detailing. Lanark is a coffee bar with particular appeal to London's coffee purists.

www.lanarkcoffee.co.uk
Hoxton

| MON-FRI. | 8:00am – 4:00pm |
| SAT-SUN. | 10:00am – 4:00pm |

First opened 2014
Roaster Alchemy and guests
Machine Victoria Arduino Athena Leva, 2 groups
Grinder Mahlkönig EK 43

Espresso	£2.00
Cappuccino	£2.50
Latte	£2.50
Flat white	£2.50

MAP REF. 160

COFFEE 4.50 / 5
OVERALL 4.25 / 5 ★★★★½

Mouse Tail

307 Whitechapel Road, E1 1BY

Mouse Tail occupies a tiny, irregular space sandwiched between Whitechapel Road and the railway lines. There's little seating inside, but what it lacks in size it makes up for in the warmth of the welcome and the quality of the coffee. It's a great place to sit and watch the action in the street market. Food is nearly all homemade at their kitchen in Clapton (sandwiches are pretty enormous), and as far as coffee is concerned, their aim is to 'do all the geeky stuff right without being intimidating.'

www.mousetailcoffee.com
⊖ Whitechapel

Sister locations Borough High Street / Canary Wharf / Canada Water

MON–FRI.	7:00am – 6:00pm
SAT–SUN.	9:00am – 5:00pm

First opened 2015
Roaster Mission Coffee Works
Machine La Marzocco PB, 2 groups
Grinder Mahlkönig Tanzania, Mazzer Kony

Espresso	£2.00
Cappuccino	£2.60
Latte	£2.60
Flat white	£2.60

 COFFEE 4.00 / 5   OVERALL 4.25 / 5

Newington Table

20 Newington Green, N16 9PU

The first thing you notice at this friendly neighbourhood eatery is the bread, baked on the premises and sold from racks inside the door. But there's a lot more to Newington Table than bread. Locals come in for excellent coffee, made using Assembly beans. They come for pastries, also baked here, and for a sit-down with friends or laptop. And they come for serious cooking, dominated by a wood-burning grill. There's a long communal table in front, with a good view of the green, and big booths along one side, some with a view of the kitchen.

+44(0)20 8617 1930
www.newingtontable.co.uk
⇌ Canonbury Rail

MON-SAT.	8:00am – 10:30pm
SUN.	8:00am – 5:00pm

First opened 2015
Roaster Assembly
Machine Nuova Simonelli Aurelia T3, 2 groups
Grinder Mahlkönig Guatemala, Nuova Simonelli Mythos One, Anfim V240

Espresso	£2.00
Cappuccino	£2.60
Latte	£2.60
Flat white	£2.50

MAP REF. 162

COFFEE 4.00 / 5	OVERALL 4.25 / 5 ★★★★⯪

Pavilion

Victoria Park, Crown Gate West, E9 7DE

Perfectly positioned overlooking a beautiful lake, Pavilion offers excellent coffee and fresh food to the crowds of locals who flock to Victoria Park every day to walk their dogs, exercise, spend time with family, or simply relax. The café itself features a striking domed glass roof and the outdoor decking area offers stunning views over the lake and park. Pavilion's popular brunch menu is organic and locally sourced wherever possible. The British-style fare is best sampled on a sunny weekend, so arrive early to avoid the queue.

⊖ Bethnal Green / Mile End

MON-SUN.	8:00am – 4:00pm

First opened 2007
Roaster Square Mile Coffee Roasters
Machine Synesso Cyncra, 3 groups
Grinder Mazzer Robur, Mazzer Super Jolly

Espresso	£2.00
Latte	£2.50
Flat white	£2.50

Sister locations Elliots / Pavilion Bakery

MAP REF. 163

COFFEE 4.25 / 5	OVERALL 4.25 / 5 ★★★★⯪

The Peanut Vendor

6 Gunmakers Lane, E3 5GG

This patch of Hackney (a lot of housing estates and light-industrial) might not seem a likely spot for a first-rate café, but that's just what The Peanut Vendor is. Staff are young, keen and friendly. They serve The Barn coffee alongside an excellent range of teas. Toasted sandwiches and baked goods dominate the small food offering. Locals come in with babies, laptops and especially dogs, which are more than welcome.

+44(0)20 8981 8613
www.thepeanutvendor.co.uk
⊖ Bow Road

MON–SUN. 9:00am – 5:30pm

First opened 2015
Roaster The Barn and guests
Machine La Marzocco Linea, 2 groups
Grinder Mazzer Major, Mahlkönig EK 43, Nuova Simonelli Mythos One

Espresso	£2.30
Cappuccino	£2.70
Latte	£2.80
Flat white	£2.70

MAP REF. 164

COFFEE 4.25 / 5

OVERALL 4.00 / 5 ★★★★☆

179

Reilly Rocket

507 Kingsland Road, E8 4AU

Situated behind a motorcycle shop, Reilly Rocket is the antidote to twee, chintzy cafés and industrial chic. Decorated with colourful memorabilia, brown leather sofas, taxidermy, and graphic wall art, Reilly's is a haven for lovers of rebellion and retro road culture. Hunter S. Thompson would have been right at home here. The coffee, pulled by a team of hardcore baristas, is just as gutsy. If you're in need of further fuel, the Antipodean-inspired brunch menu will soon have you firing on all cylinders.

+44(0)7856 433 074
www.reillyrocket.com
⊖ Dalston Junction

MON-FRI.	8:00am - 5:00pm
SAT.	9:00am - 5:00pm
SUN.	10:00am - 5:00pm

First opened 2011
Roaster Alchemy
Machine La Marzocco Linea, 2 groups
Grinder Anfim, Mahlkönig Guatemala

Espresso	£2.00
Cappuccino	£2.70
Latte	£2.60
Flat white	£2.50

MAP REF. 165

COFFEE 4.25 / 5 🫘🫘🫘🫘◐

OVERALL 4.25 / 5 ★★★★⯪

Second Shot Coffee

475 Bethnal Green Road, E2 9QH

This matchbox-size Bethnal Green newcomer is a social enterprise dedicated to working with people affected by homelessness and teaching them barista skills, hoping that they will then go on to jobs elsewhere. The coffee is noteworthy, Second Shot uses a constantly changing roster of beans. Espresso is beautifully made in their futuristic digital Nuova Simonelli. Even more enticing is the 'brewing menu', five single-origins brewed in any of three ways. Second Shot is small in size, but big in heart - and in quality.

secondshotcoffee.co.uk
⊖ Bethnal Green

MON-FRI. 7:30am - 5:00pm
SAT-SUN. 8:30am - 6:00pm

First opened 2016
Roaster Multiple roasters
Machine Nuova Simonelli Aurelia T3, 2 groups
Grinder Nuova Simonelli Mythos One, Mahlkönig EK 43

Espresso	£2.10
Cappuccino	£2.70
Latte	£2.70
Flat white	£2.60

MAP REF. **166**

COFFEE 4.25 / 5

OVERALL 3.75 / 5 ★★★★✭

181

Taylor St Baristas Canary Wharf

8 South Colonnade, Canary Wharf, E14 4PZ

This lean, mean café is designed to produce a high volume of quality coffee for the district's bankers and business people. The venue is predominantly set up to serve takeaway drinks, but there are also a small number of tables. In addition to espresso-based drinks, customers can opt for a single origin coffee brewed by AeroPress. A full breakfast menu is on offer complemented by cakes and Australian classics such as lamingtons and cheese and Vegemite muffins.

+44(0)20 7519 6536
www.taylor-st.com
⊖ Canary Wharf

Sister locations Liverpool Street / Shoreditch / Monument / Bank / Mayfair / South Quay / St Paul's

MON-FRI. 7:00am - 5:30pm
SAT-SUN. Closed

First opened 2011
Roaster Taylor St Baristas
Machine Victoria Arduino White Eagle x2
Grinder Nuova Simonelli Mythos One x3, Mazzer Robur

Espresso	£2.00
Cappuccino	£2.80 / £3.20
Latte	£2.80 / £3.20
Flat white	£2.80 / £3.70

MAP REF. 167

COFFEE 4.50 / 5	OVERALL 4.50 / 5 ★★★★✩

182

Taylor St Baristas South Quay

1 Harbour Exchange Square, E14 9GE

London's financial district runs on regular doses of caffeine, administered by the skilled hands of Taylor St's dedicated baristas. This large café offers both a rapid takeaway service and ample seating; ideal for conducting casual business meetings. The timber-clad counter is stacked with healthy salads and Antipodean treats. At South Quay, Taylor St pulls off exceptional coffee and food within the constraints of a very busy site.

+44(0)20 3069 8833
www.taylor-st.com
⊖ South Quay

Sister locations Liverpool Street / Shoreditch / Canary Wharf / Monument / Mayfair / Bank / St Paul's

MON–FRI.	7:30am – 4:30pm
SAT–SUN.	Closed

First opened 2013
Roaster Taylor St Baristas
Machine Nuova Simonelli Aurelia II T3, 3 groups
Grinder Nuova Simonelli Mythos, Mazzer Robur, Anfim, Mahlkönig Tanzania

Espresso	£1.80 / £2.30
Cappuccino	£2.50 / £2.90
Latte	£2.50 / £2.90
Flat white	£2.50 / £3.40

MAP REF. **168**

COFFEE
4.50 / 5

OVERALL
4.25 / 5

Tina, We Salute You

47 King Henry's Walk, N1 4NH

Dalston locals are fiercely protective of Tina, We Salute You. The enigmatic Tina presides over a lush selection of tarts, cakes, sticky buns, and glorious coffee. Tina's corner location provides the perfect place to soak up the afternoon sun while engrossed in a magazine. The interior is regularly given over to creatives to use as an exhibition space, and one of the outside walls hosts street art by local artists. A true local gem.

+44(0)20 3119 0047
www.tinawesaluteyou.com
⊖ Dalston Kingsland

Sister locations Stratford

MON-FRI.	8:00am - 6:00pm
SAT-SUN.	10:00am - 6:00pm

First opened 2009
Roaster Alchemy
Machine La Marzocco Linea, 2 groups
Grinder Anfim

Espresso	£2.00
Cappuccino	£2.80
Latte	£2.80
Flat white	£2.80

MAP REF. 169

COFFEE 4.25 / 5
OVERALL 4.25 / 5

Wilton Way Café

63 Wilton Way, E8 1BG

East

Wilton Way Café combines superb coffee and fresh, simple food with art and music to create a memorable experience. With its clever modular furniture, rotating art exhibits, busy coffee bar, and generous display of cakes and a radio corner producing live local broadcasts, Wilton's makes excellent use of its intimate but vibrant space. Visit on a sunny Saturday to enjoy a fine cup of coffee on the footpath outside, along with the Wilton Way faithful.

Hackney Central /
Hackney Downs Rail

MON-FRI. 8:00am - 4:30pm
SAT-SUN. 9:00am - 4:30pm

First opened 2009
Roaster Climpson & Sons
Machine La Marzocco Linea, 2 groups
Grinder Mazzer Super Jolly, Mazzer Kony

Espresso	£2.00
Cappuccino	£2.50 / £2.70
Latte	£2.50 / £2.70
Flat white	£2.50

MAP REF. 170

**COFFEE** 4.25 / 5

**OVERALL** 4.25 / 5 ★★★★☆

185

Wood St Coffee

Blackhorse Workshop, 1-2 Sutherland Road Path, E17 6BX

Walthamstow has its grimier moments, but mostly it's known for its strong community, green spaces, and, like other gentrifying areas, a growing thirst for coffee. Wood St Coffee has an authentic feel, housed in the proudly blue collar Blackhorse Workshops, busy with metalworkers, carpenters, bakers, and brewers. Come here for honest, well made coffee enjoyed with slabs of sourdough toast baked fresh on site. The building isn't easy to locate (hidden down an alley off Blackhorse Lane), but the explorer's persistence will be amply rewarded.

+44(0)7944 888 011
www.woodstcoffee.co.uk
🚇 Blackhorse Road

MON-SUN. 9:30am - 5:30pm

First opened 2014
Roaster Dark Arts Coffee and guests
Machine La Marzocco Linea, 2 groups
Grinder Mazzer Kony,
Nuova Simonelli Mythos One

Espresso	£2.00
Cappuccino	£2.40
Latte	£2.40
Flat white	£2.40

MAP REF. **171**

COFFEE 4.25 / 5

OVERALL 4.00 / 5

Yellow Warbler

9 Northwold Road, N16 7HL

This chirpy little café offers something genuinely different in N16. Venezuelan owner Andrea Boscan brings South American specialties to complement the Alchemy coffee. Try one of the scrumptious arepas, a type of flatbread made with cornflour and filled with things like guacamole, chorizo, manchego cheese, and other ingredients guaranteed to make you smile. The space is small but lively, filled with the pleasant chatter of attentive staff and their Stoke Newington regulars who flock here for the luscious food and excellent coffee.

www.yellowwarbler.co.uk
≥ Stoke Newington Rail

MON–FRI.	8:00am – 5:00pm
SAT.	9:00am – 4:30pm
SUN.	10:00am – 4:30pm

First opened 2014
Roaster Alchemy
Machine La Marzocco Linea, 2 groups
Grinder Anfim, Mazzer Super Jolly

Espresso	£2.10
Cappuccino	£2.60
Latte	£2.60
Flat white	£2.60

MAP REF. 172

COFFEE 4.25 / 5    **OVERALL** 4.25 / 5 ★★★★⯪

Zealand Road Coffee

391 Roman Road, E3 5QS

Roman Road seems an unlikely place to hunt for a good coffee. Located just a short walk away from leafy Victoria Park, Zealand Road Coffee's corner location is a natural sun-trap and the creative locals take advantage of the laid-back atmosphere to catch up on work or a good novel. Beans are supplied by Cornwall-based Origin Coffee, which has justly earned a reputation as one of the UK's premier small-batch roasters.

+44(0)7940 235 493
⊖ Mile End / Bethnal Green

MON–SAT.	8:00am – 5:00pm
SUN.	9:00am – 5:00pm

First opened 2011
Roaster Origin Coffee Roasters
Machine La Marzocco Linea, 2 groups
Grinder Mazzer Major, Compak K6

Espresso	£2.20
Cappuccino	£2.60 / £2.80
Latte	£2.60 / £2.80
Flat white	£2.60

MAP REF. 173

COFFEE 4.25 / 5    **OVERALL** 4.00 / 5 ★★★★☆

ROCKET ESPRESSO AT HOME

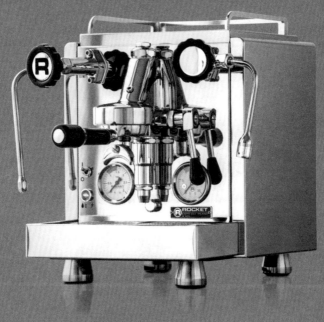

ROCKET
ESPRESSO MILANO

HANDMADE IN ITALY | ROCKET-ESPRESSO.COM

One of the capital's best kept secrets, South East London is home to a small number of quietly brilliant coffee venues, and is rapidly establishing itself on the coffee map. With the completion of the Overground line from East London to Clapham Junction via Peckham, the area is now more accessible, and rewards the urban explorer with a vibrant foodie and market scene.

South East

Anderson & Co

139 Bellenden Road, SE15 4DH

Anderson & Co was one of the first places to offer speciality coffee in a neighbourhood now in the throes of a foodie revolution. The café-restaurant complements its coffee with artisan breads, cakes, pastries, and small range of craft beer and wine. The white, bright interior serves as a perfect canvas for the medley of tastes on offer. Tantalising aromas waft from the open kitchen to the secluded outdoor seating area at the rear. Open for evening service Tuesday to Saturday, it serves up a bistro-style menu including the Peckham burger and hand-cut chips.

+44(0)20 7469 7078
www.andersonandcompany.wordpress.com
⊖ Peckham Rye

MON-SAT.	8:00am - 5:00pm
SUN.	8:30am - 4:30pm

First opened 2011
Roaster Square Mile Coffee Roasters
Machine La Marzocco Linea, 2 groups
Grinder Nuova Simonelli Mythos, Mazzer Super Jolly

Espresso	£2.00
Cappuccino	£2.60
Latte	£2.60
Flat white	£2.60

MAP REF. **174**

COFFEE 4.25 / 5	OVERALL 4.25 / 5
🫘🫘🫘🫘🫘	★★★★✫

Brick House Bakery

1 Zenoria Street, SE22 8HP

Started as a wholesale bakery in 2012, Brick House opened this retail shop and café in 2015 - and it's quickly become a local hangout. It's in a lovely space that formerly housed an electrical warehouse. The food is top-notch: made with real attention to detail. Square Mile beans are brewed in the La Marzocco Linea by a polished, friendly team. Brick House appeals to a diverse customer base with weekdays very popular with parents with babies in tow. Generous spacing of the long tables means that buggies don't get in the way.

+44(0)20 8693 2031
www.brickhousebread.com
≷ East Dulwich Rail

MON.	Closed
TUE-FRI.	8:00am - 4:00pm
SAT.	8:00am - 5:00pm
SUN.	9:00am - 5:00pm

First opened 2015
Roaster Square Mile Coffee Roasters
Machine La Marzocco Linea, 2 groups
Grinder Mazzer Robur, Mazzer Super Jolly

Espresso	£2.00
Cappuccino	£2.80
Latte	£2.80
Flat white	£2.80

MAP REF. **175**

COFFEE 4.00 / 5	OVERALL 4.25 / 5
🫘🫘🫘🫘🫘	★★★★✫

Browns of Brockley

5 Coulgate Street, SE4 2RW

Browns of Brockley is top dog for coffee in South London. Well-trained staff pull shots on an impressive Victoria Arduino Black Eagle machine, and offer single origins on filter. The simple layout and natural colour scheme create a calming atmosphere. Coffee legend and owner Ross Brown is committed to sourcing the highest quality ingredients for both coffee and food. The friendly team is completed by Ludd the pug, Browns' lovable canine mascot.

+44(0)20 8692 0722
www.brownsofbrockley.com
⊖ Brockley

| MON-FRI. | 7:30am - 4:00pm |
| SAT-SUN. | 9:00am - 4:00pm |

First opened 2009
Roaster Square Mile Coffee Roasters
Machine Victoria Arduino Black Eagle VA388, 3 groups
Grinder Mazzer Robur E, Nuova Simonelli Mythos

Espresso	£2.00
Cappuccino	£3.00
Latte	£3.20
Flat white	£3.00

MAP REF. 176

| COFFEE 4.50 / 5 | 🫘🫘🫘🫘🫘 | OVERALL 4.50 / 5 | ★★★★⯪ |

Canada Water Café

40 Surrey Quays Road, SE16 7DX

NEW

The coffee alone would make Canada Water Café worth visiting. Union's espresso blend is brewed precisely and latte art is outstanding. But the coffee's just part of the appeal of this successful venue, a combination of café, bar, and restaurant. It looks great and has a cheery vibe at busy mealtimes. The menu is wide-ranging, with an emphasis on Italian food at lunch and dinner. You get a smile and a greeting the instant you walk in the door. Those who live or work locally are fortunate. Everyone else should find a reason to pay a visit.

www.canadawatercafe.com
⊖ Canada Water

MON-FRI.	7:00am - 11:00pm
SAT.	8:30am - 11:00pm
SUN.	8:30am - 10:00pm

First opened 2014
Roaster Union Coffee Roasters
Machine Nuova Simonelli, 2 groups
Grinder Mahlkönig EK 43, Omega, Nuova Simonelli Mythos One

Espresso	£1.50
Cappuccino	£2.60
Latte	£2.80
Flat white	£2.60

MAP REF. 177

| COFFEE 4.50 / 5 | 🫘🫘🫘🫘🫘 | OVERALL 4.50 / 5 | ★★★★⯪ |

Caravan Bankside

30 Great Guildford Street, SE1 0HS

Having conquered the north with its two restaurant/cafés in Exmouth Market and King's Cross, Caravan has crossed the river to Bankside for its latest venture. This third site is big and bustling, and like the one in King's Cross it's at the centre of a thriving local scene. With offices and studios in abundant supply, there's a ready-made market for Caravan's varied, imaginative offering for both eating and drinking.

The bulk of the attractive space, in a Victorian metal box factory, is given over to tables. But there are plenty of counter seats, open for walk-ins only, for those who just want coffee and perhaps a quick bite. Their signature 'well-travelled' menu gathers in influences from all over the

globe, with an emphasis on small plates (plenty of choice for vegetarians), pizza, and home-cured meats.

On the drinks list, expect plenty of beer on tap, inventive cocktails, and more homemade activity in the form of sodas and 'shrubs.' Espresso-based drinks are always very well made at Caravan but their buying and roasting skills are best appreciated in the changing roster of single-origin filter brews.

MAP REF. **178**

COFFEE
4.50 / 5

OVERALL
4.75 / 5
★ ★ ★ ★ ✬

MON–FRI.	8:00am – 10:30pm
SAT.	10:00am – 10:30pm
SUN.	10:00am – 4.00pm

Sister locations Exmouth Market / King's Cross

First opened 2016
Roaster Caravan Coffee Roasters
Machine Faema E71
Grinder Mazzer Kold, Mahlkönig EK 43

Espresso	£2.20
Cappuccino	£2.80
Latte	£2.80
Flat white	£2.80

+44(0)20 7101 1190
www.caravanrestaurants.co.uk
⊖ Borough

The Coffee House by The Gentlemen Baristas

63 Union Street, SE1 1SG

Lords, ladies, barons, countesses and members of the general public can expect a cordial welcome at the splendid premises of 63 Union Street. The building itself boasts a fascinating history: it originally housed one of London's oldest coffee roasteries dating back to the 18th century. Proprietors Henry Ayers and Edward Parkes, two tweed-clad coffee chaps, have also set up a coffee training school in the space above the shop. The coffee here is really rather spiffing, but owners of particularly dashing moustaches should exercise caution when indulging in cappuccinos.

+44(0)7817 350 067
www.thegentlemenbaristas.com
⊖ Borough / London Bridge

Sister locations Store Street

MON-FRI.	7:00am - 6:00pm
SAT.	8:30am - 5:00pm
SUN.	9:30am - 4:00pm

First opened 2014
Roaster Wogan, Department of Coffee, Neighbourhood
Machine Faema E71, 3 groups
Grinder Nuova Simonelli Mythos x2, Mazzer Kold, Mazzer Mini E

Espresso	£2.00
Cappuccino	£2.60 / £2.80
Latte	£2.60 / £2.80
Flat white	£2.70

MAP REF. 179

COFFEE
4.50 / 5

OVERALL
4.25 / 5

The Coffee Works Project
Blackfriars Road 235 Blackfriars Road, SE1 8BF

This Coffee Works Project on Blackfriars Road couldn't be more different from their other venues, in Leadenhall Market and Angel. When you walk up to the counter, you'll begin by gabbing with the disarmingly friendly staff. But then it's down to business. The Coffee Works Project espresso from their fully manual Slayer is flawless, with textbook crema and just the right extraction for a beautifully balanced cup. Food arrives daily from a central kitchen, and everything's made in-house except bread and pastries. Locals, whether in jeans or suits, have already spotted the quality.

+44(0)20 7928 8456
www.coffeeworksproject.com
⊖ Southwark

Sister locations Angel / Leadenhall

MON–FRI.	7:30am – 5:00pm
SAT–SUN.	Closed

First opened 2015
Roaster The Coffee Works Project
Machine Slayer V3, 3 groups
Grinder Nuova Simonelli Mythos x2, Mahlkönig EK 43

Espresso	£2.20
Cappuccino	£2.80
Latte	£2.80
Flat white	£2.80

MAP REF. **180**

Coleman Coffee

20 Lower Marsh, SE1 7RJ

Jack Coleman has worked in the coffee business, one way or another, since he was thirteen. Perhaps that explains the complete self-confidence in every aspect of his first retail outlet. This half-pint-size café uses only full-fat Jersey milk, doesn't have loyalty cards or Wi-Fi, and serves a specialised food offering centred around Staffordshire oatcakes (sweet and savoury). It's all about the coffee here: excellent beans, expertly brewed, from a venerable Synesso or filter. Try their 'old-fashioned espresso'. And in good weather, drink it in a lovely back garden which boasts both a pomegranate tree and a mulberry tree.

+44(0)20 3267 1139

⊖ Waterloo / Lambeth North

| MON-FRI. | 8:00am – 3:00pm |
| SAT-SUN. | 9:30am – 3:00pm |

First opened 2016
Roaster Coleman Coffee
Machine Synesso Cyncra, 3 groups
Grinder Mazzer Kony E, Ditting

Espresso	£2.00
Cappuccino	£2.60
Latte	£2.70
Flat white	£2.60

MAP REF. **181**

COFFEE
4.50 / 5

OVERALL
4.25 / 5 ★★★★½

Daily Goods

36 Camberwell Church Street, SE5 8QZ

Relocating from the concession at Kinoko Cycles, Daily Goods is a much needed shot in the arm for Camberwell's café scene. Run by Carter Donnell, who practised his craft at New York's renowned Ninth Street Espresso, Daily Goods has a relaxed atmosphere attracting a cross-section of Camberwell residents. In a doff of the (baseball) cap to Yankee coffee culture, the menu includes filter coffee served in American diner-style mugs. But forget any preconceptions you might have about bulk brew; the baristas at Daily Goods are anything but casual about their coffee.

www.dailygoodslondon.co.uk
⊖ Denmark Hill

MON–FRI. 7:30am – 5:00pm
SAT–SUN. 8:30am – 5:00pm

First opened 2014
Roaster Daily Goods, Caravan, Quarter Horse, Square Mile, Round Hill
Machine La Marzocco Linea, 2 groups
Grinder Nuova Simonelli Mythos One

Espresso	£2.20
Cappuccino	£2.60
Latte	£2.60
Flat white	£2.60

MAP REF. 182

 COFFEE 4.50 / 5   **OVERALL** 4.25 / 5 ★ ★ ★ ★ ⯪

FCB Coffee

Denmark Hill Station, Windsor Walk, SE5 8BB

 NEW

Talk about location! FCB sits literally on top of a busy commuter rail station and a three-minute walk from a busy teaching hospital. For several hours in the morning they operate a dedicated La Marzocco selling takeaway coffees from the window. Even when things quiet down, it can still be a lively, humming place. They sell good sandwiches, and people come to eat them here - as well as drink carefully brewed coffees from Horsham and rotating guests - at the small handful of tables.

www.fcbcoffee.com
⇌ Denmark Hill Rail

MON–FRI. 6:00am – 8:00pm
SAT. 7:00am – 7:00pm
SUN. 8:30am – 4:00pm

First opened 2014
Roaster Horsham Coffee Roaster and guests
Machine La Marzocco Linea AV, 2 groups
Grinder Mahlkönig EK 43, La Marzocco Volcano, Ceado E37, Ceado E7

Espresso	£1.70
Cappuccino	£2.40
Latte	£2.40
Flat white	£2.40

MAP REF. 183

COFFEE 4.00 / 5 **OVERALL** 3.75 / 5 ★ ★ ★ ⯪ ☆

Fee & Brown

50 High Street, Beckenham, BR3 1AY

Fee & Brown sets a new benchmark for coffee in London's suburbs. Husband and wife team Ercan and Del serve a Climpson & Sons' blend. The artisan lunch menu, ample space, and plentiful seating make Fee & Brown an excellent choice for groups. Baked treats fill the counter top, and whole cakes are available to order. The café's dedication to quality coffee is resolutely upheld by the team of passionate young baristas.

+44(0)20 8658 1996
www.feeandbrown.com
≥ Beckenham Junction Rail

MON-FRI.	7:30am – 4:30pm
SAT.	9:00am – 5:00pm
SUN.	10:00am – 4:00pm

First opened 2012
Roaster Climpson & Sons
Machine La Marzocco Linea, 2 groups
Grinder Mazzer Robur x2

Espresso	£2.20
Cappuccino	£2.60
Latte	£2.60
Flat white	£2.60

MAP REF. 184

COFFEE
4.25 / 5

OVERALL
4.50 / 5

★★★★✦

Four Corners Cafe

12 Lower Marsh, SE1 7RJ

Four Corners is a bright, quirky café decorated with posters bearing punchy coffee-related puns and littered with travel magazines and paraphernalia. Owner Gary Baxter's vision puts it as a crossroads, halfway between a coffee shop and hostel, a place for people who are coming, going, or just dreaming of their next big adventure. While you plan your travels, whether to Sydenham or Sydney, enjoy a coffee made with Ozone beans, pulled on a La Marzocco Linea, and a buttery, to-die-for pastry.

+44(0)20 8617 9591
www.four-corners-cafe.com
⊖ Waterloo / Lambeth North

MON-FRI.	7:30am - 6:30pm
SAT.	9:00am - 5:00pm
SUN.	Closed

First opened 2013
Roaster Ozone Coffee Roasters
Machine La Marzocco Linea, 2 groups
Grinder Mazzer Luigi

Espresso	£2.00
Cappuccino	£2.60
Latte	£2.60
Flat white	£2.60

MAP REF. 185

COFFEE 4.00 / 5	OVERALL 4.25 / 5 ★★★★☆

Fowlds Cafe

3 Addington Square, SE5 7JZ

Tucked away on bohemian Addington Square, this charming little café is a collaboration with Fowlds upholstery firm, occupying the site since 1926. This family business continues to operate from the rear of the property, while the shopfront is given over to coffee and cake. The workshop itself is occasionally repurposed for atmospheric candle-lit supper clubs. Fowlds' beautiful old-fashioned shop sign hangs from the facade, casting an enchanting spell over this forgotten corner of Camberwell. Fowlds is a quietly brilliant coffee spot well worth a detour to visit.

+44(0)20 3417 4500
Oval / Kennington

Sister locations Louie Louie

MON-FRI.	7:30am – 5:00pm
SAT.	8:30am – 5:00pm
SUN.	9:00am – 4:00pm

First opened 2014
Roaster Square Mile Coffee Roasters
Machine La Marzocco Linea, 2 groups
Grinder Anfim

Espresso	£2.10
Cappuccino	£2.70
Latte	£2.70
Flat white	£2.70

MAP REF. 186

COFFEE 4.00 / 5 — OVERALL 4.25 / 5 ★★★★☆

General Store

174 Bellenden Road, SE15 4BW

General Store is one of a rare breed of delicatessens with a real understanding of speciality coffee. Workshop espresso is expertly pulled from a La Marzocco by friendly staff. The owners' passion for quality food and drink is abundantly clear in the irresistible range of provisions filling the shelves: fresh fruit and vegetables, dry goods, cured meats and cheeses. All produce is selected with an exceptionally keen eye for provenance and seasonality. Complement your coffee with a mouth-watering pastry.

+44(0)20 7642 2129
www.generalsto.re
Peckham Rye

MON-TUE.	Closed
WED-FRI.	9:00am – 7:00pm
SAT.	8:00am – 6:00pm
SUN.	9:00am – 5:00pm

First opened 2013
Roaster Workshop Coffee
Machine La Marzocco Linea, 2 groups
Grinder Mazzer Super Jolly

Espresso	£2.00
Cappuccino	£2.60
Latte	£2.60
Flat white	£2.60

MAP REF. 187

COFFEE 4.25 / 5 — OVERALL 4.25 / 5 ★★★★☆

The Hub Coffee House

Oasis Centre, 1a Kennington Road, SE1 7QP

Hub is part of the Oasis Waterloo group, which provides services for the local community including food banks and debt advice. It is an admirable organisation in every way. But if you're expecting Hub to be a dreary place (especially since it shares a building with a public library), you're dead wrong. This is a lively local, good-looking and eminently hipster-friendly. The house espresso blend is best drunk with milk, or there's single-origin filter. If you have a sweet tooth, make sure to feed it a cookie or a wicked slice of cake.

+44(0)20 3267 4214
www.hubcoffeehouse.org
⊖ Lambeth North / Waterloo

MON–FRI.	8:00am – 6:00pm
SAT.	9:30am – 5:00pm
SUN.	9:30am – 11:00am

First opened 2016
Roaster Kingdom Coffee
Machine Iberital Expressions
Grinder Mazzer Jolly

Espresso	£1.70
Cappuccino	£2.20
Latte	£2.20
Flat white	£2.50

MAP REF. 188

COFFEE 4.00 / 5	🫘🫘🫘🫘🫘	OVERALL 4.25 / 5	★★★★✩

London Grind

2 London Bridge, SE1 9RA

Most people come here for the delicious food, though the Grind house espresso is of a high standard. London Grind focuses on delivering good food and a lively, perfectly boisterous vibe. And it's doing the job right, it seems. The place attracts crowds from nearby offices and from Borough Market (a coffee bean's throw away). Come for coffee and lunch during the day, by all means. In the evening you may prefer a Hot Flat White Russian: espresso, vodka, Kahlua and milk.

+44(0)20 7378 1928
www.londongrind.com
 London Bridge

Sister locations Clerkenwell / Covent Garden / Holborn / Royal Exchange / Shoreditch / Soho / Exmouth Market / Whitechapel

MON–THU.	7:00am – 12:00am
FRI	7:00am – 1:00am
SAT.	8:00am – 1:00am
SUN.	9:00am – 7:00pm

First opened 2015
Roaster The Grind House Espresso
Machine La Marzocco Linea PB, 2 groups x2
Grinder Nuova Simonelli Mythos One x3, Mahlkönig Tanzania

Espresso	£2.20
Cappuccino	£2.90
Latte	£2.90
Flat white	£2.80

MAP REF. 189

COFFEE 4.25 / 5	OVERALL 4.25 / 5

Monmouth Coffee Company Borough

2 Park Street, SE1 9AB

Monmouth Coffee Company has developed a cult-like following among many Londoners who make weekly pilgrimages to this coffee mecca. The Borough Market venue, larger than the Covent Garden premises, is incredibly popular with market regulars and tourists, and is appropriately surrounded by some of the city's finest producers of foods and beverages. Fridays and Saturdays are extremely busy, so a weekday trip is a safer bet. Also worth a visit is Monmouth's Bermondsey outpost, at Arch 3 Spa North, open Saturdays only 9:00am - 1:30pm.

+44(0)20 7232 3010
www.monmouthcoffee.co.uk
⊖ London Bridge

MON.-SAT.	7:30am - 6:00pm
SUN.	Closed

First opened 2001
Roaster Monmouth Coffee Company
Machine La Marzocco Linea, 2 groups x2
Grinder Mazzer Robur x2

Espresso	£1.70
Cappuccino	£2.70
Latte	£2.70
Flat white	£2.70

Sister locations Covent Garden / Bermondsey

MAP REF. 190

COFFEE 4.50 / 5		OVERALL 4.50 / 5	★★★★⯨

No67 at South London Gallery

67 Peckham Road, SE5 8UH

Set within a handsome townhouse adjoining the South London Gallery, No67 is a popular café and dining room frequently packed out for weekend brunch. At less busy periods it offers a soothing respite from the din of busy Camberwell.
The house espresso blend is handled well, and makes an excellent complement to the outstanding Full Spanglish breakfast. Open well into the evening, No67 is also an ideal spot to enjoy great wine, cocktails and craft beer with the cultured South London crowd.

+44(0)20 7252 7649
www.number67.co.uk
⊖ Peckham Rye / Denmark Hill

MON.	Closed
TUE.	8:00am - 6:30pm
WED.-FRI.	8:00am - 11:00pm
SAT.	10:00am - 11:00pm
SUN.	10:00am - 6:30pm

First opened 2010
Roaster House espresso blend
Machine La Marzocco FB/80, 2 groups
Grinder Nuova Simonelli Mythos One

Espresso	£1.50 / £1.80
Cappuccino	£2.50 / £2.80
Latte	£2.50 / £2.80
Flat white	£2.50 / £2.80

MAP REF. 191

COFFEE 4.25 / 5		OVERALL 4.25 / 5	★★★★⯨

Old Spike Roastery

54 Peckham Rye, SE15 4JR

Old Spike would be an admirable outfit even if it didn't make good coffee. It was founded in 2015 as a social enterprise aimed at helping people cope with homelessness by training them in the coffee trade. And in providing that training, it has also laid the foundation for its own growth. At the time this edition of the LCG was being compiled, their roasting programme was being expanded considerably. This tiny café remains the showcase for their beans, all of them presented as single-origin and therefore a good candidate for ordering from a filter.

www.oldspikeroastery.com

⊖ Peckham Rye

MON.	Closed
TUE.-FRI.	7:30am – 3:00pm
SAT.-SUN.	9:30am – 5:00pm

First opened 2015
Roaster Old Spike Roastery
Machine La Cimbali M28
Grinder Anfim Super Caimano, Ditting KR1403

Espresso	£2.00
Cappuccino	£2.50
Latte	£2.50
Flat white	£2.50

MAP REF.

   COFFEE 4.00 / 5

 OVERALL 3.75 / 5

Red Lion Coffee Co.

Corner of Batavia Road and Clifton Rise, SE14 6AX

Red Lion gets everything right in a compact space just a few minutes away from both Fordham Park and Goldsmiths College. If it looks a bit like a Department of Coffee and Social Affairs, that's because the owner used to work there. Coffee is all from Climpsons beans and the espresso blend shows at its best with beautifully decorated milk on top. There are sweet and savoury baked goods to eat, hot dishes of the day, and small selections of beer and wine. An oasis of good coffee in New Cross, Red Lion looks set to be a roaring success.

www.redlioncoffee.co.uk
⊖ New Cross Gate

MON–SUN. 8:00am – 9:00pm

First opened 2016
Roaster Climpson & Sons
Machine La Marzocco Linea PB, 2 groups
Grinder Nuova Simonelli Mythos One, Mazzer Super Jolly

Espresso	£1.80
Cappuccino	£2.80
Latte	£2.80
Flat white	£2.80

MAP REF. **193**

COFFEE
4.25 / 5

OVERALL
4.00 / 5 ★★★★☆

Small White Elephant

28 Choumert Road, SE15 4SE

For those days when you're furious with the world, we prescribe a trip to Small White Elephant. This café is a calming sanctuary run by Dale Carney and Jehn Richardson, two of the nicest people ever to open a coffee shop. Let us count the ways they will make you smile: local art on the walls, a veritable jungle of plants, tasty Alchemy coffee, and even monthly jazz and poetry nights. We must also mention the French toast. This is the real deal, triumphant coconutty slabs saturated in syrup. Whatever your day has thrown at you, Small White Elephant has a remedy.

www.smallwhiteelephant.com
🚇 Peckham Rye

MON–FRI.	9:00am – 5:30pm
SAT.	9:30am – 5:00pm
SUN.	10:00am – 5:00pm

First opened 2014
Roaster Alchemy, Extract Coffee Roasters
Machine La Marzocco GB5, 2 groups
Grinder Mazzer Super Jolly

Espresso	£2.10
Cappuccino	£2.60
Latte	£2.80
Flat white	£2.60

MAP REF. 194

COFFEE 4.25 / 5

OVERALL 4.25 / 5 ★★★★⯪

St. David Coffee House

5 David's Road, SE23 3EP

St. David Coffee House brims with retro charm. Local artists, actors, musicians, and families come in droves to sip espresso among the books, stacks of vinyl, and vintage movie memorabilia. The owners host regular events, such as pizza nights in collaboration with sourdough pizza purveyors Van Dough. This isn't a café which is trying hard to be liked; the atmosphere feels welcoming and uncontrived. Its easy-going nature and strong community links have made it very much part of Forest Hill life.

+44(0)20 8291 6646
⊖ Forest Hill

MON.	Closed
TUE-WED.	8:00am - 5:00pm
THU-FRI.	8:00am - 11:00pm
SAT.	9:00am - 5:00pm
SUN.	10:00am - 4:00pm

First opened 2010
Roaster Square Mile Coffee Roasters and guests
Machine Rancilio Classe 10, 2 groups
Grinder Anfim

Espresso	£2.00
Cappuccino	£2.50
Latte	£2.50
Flat white	£2.40

MAP REF. 195

 COFFEE 4.00 / 5   OVERALL 4.00 / 5

Tate Boiler House Kitchen and Bar

Tate Modern, Bankside, SE1 9TG

The view of St Paul's is enough to make a visit to Tate Kitchen and Bar worthwhile. But it's not the only reason to come here. Using the Tate's own beans, the baristas brew up fabulous drinks in their pair of gleaming Modbars and in filter. The house espresso blend is sweet and rounded enough to drink without sugar or milk, though the milky versions are extremely well made. Enjoy them after a meal (the cooking is simple but well done) or in one of the comfortable seats by the window. Which is closer, of course, to That View.

www.tate.org.uk/visit/tate-modern/kitchen-and-bar

⊖ Blackfriars

SUN–FRI.	10:00am – 5:30pm
SAT.	10:00am – 5:30pm

First opened 2016
Roaster Tate
Machine Modbar, 2 groups
Grinder Mahlkönig K30

Espresso	£2.55
Cappuccino	£3.35
Latte	£3.35
Flat white	£3.45

MAP REF. 196

COFFEE 4.25 / 5
OVERALL 4.50 / 5 ★★★★✬

Volcano Coffee House

Parkhall Trading Estate, 40 Martell Road, SE21 8EN

South East

Volcano operates from a former electronics factory, surprisingly located among a row of terraced houses. This architecturally impressive building houses the roastery and a spacious café. Opt for Volcano's own 'Fullsteam' espresso blend, or try a range of single-estate filters. A collection of antique coffee machines and a vintage roaster displayed on gallery-style plinths announce the founders' shared love for classic machinery. Volcano resonates with a deep passion for espresso culture, past and present.

+44(0)20 8761 8415
www.volcanocoffeeworks.com
⇌ West Norwood Rail / West Dulwich Rail

MON-FRI.	8:00am - 4:00pm
SAT.	9:00am - 4:00pm
SUN.	Closed

First opened 2012
Roaster Volcano Coffee Works
Machine La Marzocco Linea, 3 groups
Grinder Mazzer Kold, Mazzer Super Jolly

Espresso	£2.20
Cappuccino	£2.40
Latte	£2.40
Flat white	£2.40

MAP REF. 197

COFFEE 4.75 / 5	🫘🫘🫘🫘🫘	OVERALL 4.50 / 5	★★★★⯪

The Watch House

199 Bermondsey Street, SE1 3UW

During the nineteenth century, the fascinating Watch House building housed guards protecting the churchyard of St Mary Magdalen against body-snatchers. This unique octagonal space has been transformed into a cosy retreat complete with rustic wooden lampshades, underfloor heating, and even a wood-burning hearth. Happily, the Watch House doesn't disappoint Bermondsey Street's discerning food lovers. In addition to hand-roasted Ozone coffee, the counter is stacked high with homemade sandwiches and indulgent goodies.

+44(0)20 7407 6431
www.watchhousecoffee.com
⊖ London Bridge

MON–FRI.	7:00am – 6:00pm
SAT–SUN.	8:00am – 6:00pm

First opened 2014
Roaster Ozone Coffee Roasters
Machine La Marzocco Linea PB, 2 groups
Grinder Mazzer Major, Mahlkönig EK 43

Espresso	£2.20
Cappuccino	£2.70
Latte	£2.70
Flat white	£2.50

MAP REF. 198

COFFEE 4.00 / 5

OVERALL 4.25 / 5 ★★★★⯪

South West London contains a dizzying array of cultural influences, from the Afro-Caribbean heritage of Brixton to the Antipodean-influenced lifestyle of Clapham and the genteel suburban rhythms of Putney. The area's colourful and creative coffee culture reflects these unique influences and local quirks.

South West

Artisan East Sheen

139 Sheen Lane, SW14 8LR

Artisan's East Sheen location occupies a great spot, with light flooding in through huge windows. The recycled wood décor will put a smile on your face. Behind the big counter, the baristas know just what to do with Allpress beans – and with textured milk, too. But the greatest thing is the warm and welcome feel. The owners say this area has a distinctive village feel, and 'a lot of customers bring their cups and plates up to the counter when they're finished.' Just like home.

+44(0)20 8617 3477
www.artisancoffee.co.uk
⊖ Mortlake

Sister locations Ealing / Stamford Brook / Putney

MON–FRI.	7:30am – 5:00pm
SAT.	8:00am – 5:00pm
SUN.	8:30am – 5:00pm

First opened 2015
Roaster Allpress Espresso, The Barn
Machine La Marzocco FB/80, 3 groups
Grinder Nuova Simonelli Mythos One, Mazzer Super Jolly

Espresso	£2.20
Cappuccino	£2.60 / £2.90
Latte	£2.60 / £2.90
Flat white	£2.60 / £2.90

MAP REF. 199

| COFFEE | OVERALL |
| 4.50 / 5 | 4.50 / 5 ★★★★✦ |

Artisan Putney

203 Upper Richmond Road, SW15 6SG

Artisan's motto, 'we are obsessively passionate about coffee', is an apt philosophy for this busy café. The Putney site and its sister venues benefit from advanced water filtration systems and serve beautiful single origin coffees from guest roasters. The warm, light-filled space is furnished with quirky furniture, and the inventive loyalty scheme encourages customers to spin a wheel of fortune which determines their reward. Everyone from mums with prams to picky coffee geeks will be met by a genuinely warm welcome and superb coffee.

+44(0)20 8617 3477
www.artisancoffee.co.uk
⊖ East Putney / ⇌ Putney Rail

Sister locations Ealing / Stamford Brook / East Sheen

MON–FRI.	7:00am – 6:00pm
SAT.	8:00am – 6:00pm
SUN.	8:30am – 6:00pm

First opened 2011
Roaster Allpress Espresso, The Barn
Machine La Marzocco FB/80, 3 groups
Grinder Nuova Simonelli Mythos One

Espresso	£2.20
Cappuccino	£2.60 / £2.90
Latte	£2.60 / £2.90
Flat white	£2.60 / £2.90

MAP REF. **200**

COFFEE 4.50 / 5		OVERALL 4.50 / 5	

217

Batch & Co Coffee

54 Streatham Hill, SW2 4RD

Jen Batchelor, the owner of Batch, wants it to be a community centre - her background is in social enterprise and community work. But there's a lot more to Batch than good intentions: this is a great local. The food is great, with sandwiches, toasties, and pastries all strong points, and they've got Caravan to roast a bespoke espresso blend for them. If you're dawdling a while in the 'lending library' at the back, a V60 from the changing selection of single-origin beans may be your drink of choice.

+44(0)20 8616 6767
www.batchandco.com
⊖ Brixton

MON-FRI.	9:00am - 5:30pm
SAT.	9:00am - 5:00pm
SUN.	10:00am - 4:00pm

First opened 2016
Roaster Caravan Coffee Roasters
Machine La Marzocco Linea, 2 groups
Grinder Mazzer Robur, Mazzer Super Jolly

Espresso	£2.20
Cappuccino	£2.70
Latte	£2.70
Flat white	£2.50

MAP REF. 201

COFFEE 4.25 / 5

OVERALL 4.00 / 5 ★★★★☆

Birdhouse

123 St John's Hill, SW11 1SZ

This perfectly formed café is a striking addition to St John's Hill. The interior is light, beautifully furnished in brushed steel and vintage wood, punctuated with splashes of bright yellow. Bird images and other avian touches create a unique experience, and an old carpenter's work block serves a new duty as a coffee bar. At weekends Birdhouse is a flurry of activity as plates of steaming baked eggs and beautifully-poured flat whites make their way to brunching Battersea locals.

+44(0)20 7228 6663
www.birdhou.se
⊖ Clapham Junction

MON-FRI. 7:00am - 4:00pm
SAT-SUN. 9:00am - 5:00pm

First opened 2011
Roaster Climpson & Sons
Machine La Marzocco Linea, 3 groups
Grinder Anfim, Mazzer Robur E

Espresso	£2.20
Cappuccino	£2.60 / £2.90
Latte	£2.60 / £2.90
Flat white	£2.60

MAP REF. 202

COFFEE 4.50 / 5 **OVERALL** 4.25 / 5 ★★★★⯪

The Black Lab Coffee House

18 Clapham Common Southside, SW4 7AB

The recently refurbished Black Lab Coffee House is a warm and cosy place to enjoy your coffee. The venue has comfortable seating and is a great place to catch up with friends, but can fill up rapidly at weekends. Black Lab has a great coffee offering with a roster including Alchemy, Round Hill and Square Mile. They also offer a range of home brewing gear and beans ground to order. Single estate coffees brewed by AeroPress are also offered at less busy periods.

+44(0)20 7738 8441
www.blacklabcoffee.com
⊖ Clapham Common

MON-FRI.	7:00am - 5:00pm
SAT.	8:00am - 4:30pm
SUN.	9:00am - 4:30pm

First opened 2010
Roaster 8 rotating UK roasters
Machine La Marzocco Linea PB, 2 groups
Grinder Mazzer Kony x2, Nuova Simonelli Mythos One x2, Mahlkönig EK 43

Espresso	£2.00
Cappuccino	£2.80
Latte	£2.70
Flat white	£2.60

MAP REF. **203**

COFFEE 4.25 / 5

OVERALL 4.25 / 5 ★★★★⯪

Brew

45 Northcote Road, SW11 1NJ

A favourite with the Northcote Road set, Brew is a cheerful antidote to the many chain coffee stores nearby. Simple and cosy, Brew offers a comprehensive menu in a breezy, laidback environment. However, this café is best known for its sensational breakfasts, which feature only the best quality local ingredients, as well as juices and smoothies. A tantalising beer and wine list is also on offer.

+44(0)20 7585 2198
www.brew-cafe.com
⊖ Clapham Junction

Sister locations Wimbledon / Putney / Wandsworth / Chiswick

TUE-SAT.	7:00am - 10:00pm
SUN-MON.	7:00am - 6:00pm

First opened 2008
Roaster Allpress Espresso
Machine La Marzocco Linea, 2 groups
Grinder Mazzer Super Jolly

Espresso	£2.30 / £2.60
Cappuccino	£2.90
Latte	£2.90
Flat white	£2.90

MAP REF. 204

COFFEE 4.00 / 5		OVERALL 4.25 / 5	★★★★⯪

Brickwood Balham

11 Hildreth Street, SW12 9RQ

This place looks outstanding. Corrugated steel, distressed woods and recycled coffee bags dominate the décor - you can almost imagine you're riding the rails in a 1930s American black-and-white movie. If the appearance is rugged, the coffee and service are smooth and polished. The Brickwood interpretation of Caravan's blend produces great results, crema standing proud in a little glass beaker. All the food for the three branches is cooked here, so it's always in tiptop shape - like everything else at this lovely hangout.

+44(0)20 8772 6818
www.brickwoodlondon.com
⊖ Balham

MON-FRI.	7:00am - 6:00pm
SAT-SUN.	9:00am - 6:00pm

First opened 2015
Roaster Caravan Coffee Roasters
Machine La Marzocco FB70, 2 groups
Grinder Mazzer Robur

Espresso £2.50
Cappuccino £2.70
Latte £2.70
Flat white £2.70

Sister locations Clapham / Tooting

MAP REF. 205

COFFEE 4.25 / 5		OVERALL 4.25 / 5	★★★★

Brickwood Clapham

16 Clapham Common South Side, SW4 7AB

Brickwood brings proper Aussie-style coffee and brunches to Clapham. Corn fritters with a choice of hallumi and poached egg, or avocado and chorizo ought to sort you out after a heavy Friday night. With an outdoor courtyard at the rear, visitors can enjoy their sunny Antipodean brunch under a (hopefully!) bright English sky. The punchy Caravan coffee perfectly complements the food's bold flavours, and is confidently prepared by enthusiastic baristas on a stunning mint green La Marzocco, affectionately nicknamed 'Lola'.

+44(0)20 7819 9614
www.brickwoodlondon.com
⊖ Clapham Common

Sister locations Balham / Tooting

MON-FRI.	7:00am - 6:00pm
SAT-SUN.	9:00am - 6:00pm

First opened 2013
Roaster Caravan Coffee Roasters
Machine La Marzocco FB/80, 2 groups
Grinder Mazzer Luigi

Espresso	£2.30
Cappuccino	£2.70
Latte	£2.70
Flat white	£2.70

MAP REF.

COFFEE 4.25 / 5	OVERALL 4.50 / 5
🫘🫘🫘🫘🫘	★★★★★

Brickwood Tooting

21 Tooting High Street, SW17 0SN

The newest of the Brickwood venues, this corner spot in Tooting Market has become a hugely popular destination for weekend breakfast/brunch/lunch. Be prepared for queues, in other words. Weekdays are quieter, but there may still be a good lunchtime crowd: friends of all ages, sometimes with babies in tow, eating toasties, eggs or salads. Brickwood's variation on the Caravan espresso blend produces a cup with fine red-berry sweetness, a perfect companion while you watch market life pass before your eyes.

+44(0)20 7819 9614
www.brickwoodlondon.com
⊖ Tooting Broadway

Sister locations Clapham / Balham

MON-SUN. 9:00am - 5:00pm

First opened 2015
Roaster Caravan Coffee Roasters
Machine La Marzocco FB/70, 2 groups
Grinder Mazzer Luigi

Espresso	£2.30
Cappuccino	£2.70
Latte	£2.70
Flat white	£2.70

MAP REF.

COFFEE 4.25 / 5		OVERALL 4.25 / 5	★★★★⯪

223

Brixton Blend

8 Tunstall Road, SW9 8BN

Brixton Blend sits bang opposite the David Bowie mural, and it's a welcome indie in an area dominated by chains. Expect three things here: a nice-looking space, friendly service, and excellent coffee - some of the best latte art we've seen this year floated on a BB latte. You'll be offered your choice of Nude or Volcano for an espresso-based drink, a nice touch. The coffee comes only in cardboard even for drinking in, as the spiral staircase to the first floor is very steep. Cardboard is a price worth paying for coffee of this quality.

+44(0)20 7733 0775
www.brixtonblend.co.uk
⊖ Brixton

Sister locations Brockwell Blend

MON-FRI.	6:30am - 6:00pm
SAT-SUN.	8:00am - 6:00pm

First opened 2016
Roaster Nude Coffee Roasters, Volcano Coffee Works
Machine La Marzocco GB5, 3 groups
Grinder Nuova Simonelli Mythos One, Mazzer Mini, Mahlkönig EK 43

Espresso	£2.00
Cappuccino	£2.70
Latte	£2.70
Flat white	£2.70

MAP REF. 208

COFFEE 4.25 / 5	OVERALL 4.00 / 5	★★★★☆

Brockwell Blend

19 Tulse Hill, SW2 2TH

South West

This sister café to Brixton Blend has a great location just a few minutes away from Brockwell Park. Locals going for a walk in the greenery can (and do) stop in to fetch something hot to drink while they exercise Pooch or the kiddies. But it's worth dawdling here, too. The space is attractive, the WiFi's good, and there's outdoor seating in back. Not to mention some good sandwiches (bagels are a strong point) and extremely well made coffees, all espresso-based, from Nude and Volcano.

www.brockwellblend.co.uk
Brixton

Sister locations Brixton Blend

MON–FRI.	7:00am – 4:30pm
SAT.	8:00am – 6:00pm
SUN.	9:30am – 4:30pm

First opened 2016
Roaster Nude Coffee Roasters, Volcano Coffee Works
Machine La Marzocco GB, 2 groups
Grinder Nuova Simonelli Mythos One

Espresso	£2.00
Cappuccino	£2.70
Latte	£2.70
Flat white	£2.70

MAP REF. 209

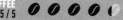
COFFEE 4.25 / 5

OVERALL 4.25 / 5 ★★★★

225

Brother Marcus

9 Chestnut Grove, SW12 8JA

Brother Marcus is a lively local with very friendly baristas. Beans come from Caravan and keep the La Marzocco Linea working hard throughout the day. Food focuses on brunch dishes with some excruciatingly punning names, which you can enjoy with a cocktail if you're brave, while the evenings often feature popup supper clubs. (They're very popular; book well in advance.) And check out their hidden garden out the back, a lovely retreat. Brother Marcus sits less than 50 metres away from Balham station, so it's also a good place to pick up your pick-me-up before the morning commute.

brothermarcus.co.uk

⊖ Balham

MON-TUE.	8:00am – 4:30pm
WED-FRI.	8:00am – 11:30pm
SAT.	9:00am – 11:30pm
SUN.	9:30am – 4:00pm

UK COFFEE WEEK

First opened 2016
Roaster Caravan Coffee Roasters
Machine La Marzocco Linea, 2 groups
Grinder Mazzer

Espresso	£2.00
Cappuccino	£2.40
Latte	£2.40
Flat white	£2.40

MAP REF.

COFFEE
4.25 / 5

OVERALL
4.00 / 5

Café Fleur

198 St Ann's Hill, SW18 2RT

Many of London's cafés buy in at least part of the food they serve, especially baked stuff, but at Café Fleur it's 100 per cent home-made. They'll even bake you birthday and wedding cakes if you want one. But you can also just settle down with breakfast or lunch, perhaps with a glass of organic wine or craft beer. The coffee comes from Brixton's own Volcano roastery, and it's served up by a friendly team with some particularly lovely latte art in evidence.

www.cafefleurwandsworth.com

⊖ Wandsworth Common

MON-FRI.	8:00am - 5:00pm
SAT-SUN.	9:00am - 6:00pm

First opened 2014
Roaster Volcano Coffee Works
Machine La Marzocco FB/80. 2 groups
Grinder Nuova Simonelli Mythos One

Espresso	£2.00
Cappuccino	£2.20
Latte	£2.20
Flat white	£2.20

MAP REF. 211

COFFEE 4.00 / 5

OVERALL 4.25 / 5 ★★★★⯪

227

Caya

344 Coldharbour Lane, SW9 8QH

We've all been there. You walk into a café that's heaving with customers, yet there is complete silence. Why? Because every chair is occupied by someone working on their laptop and never talking to anyone else. And the owner may be wondering how they're going to pay the rent when some customers stay for three hours and order just a single latte.

Caya has devised a neat solution to the dilemma. Set away from the centre of Brixton's lively scene, Caya is an attractive place with two separate areas: a café at the front and a custom-made 'work space' at the back with a long table, electrical outlets, and WiFi that promises blazing-fast speeds. You rent space in back by the

hour or the day, with bottomless coffee or tea, so you get your workspace for a very reasonable rent. If you're just relaxing, however, the comfortable front area is a lovely place to enjoy Ozone's espresso blend (best with milk) or a single-origin filter. Who knows, you may enjoy yourself so much that you go back with friends and actually talk to them.

MAP REF. 212

| COFFEE 4.25 / 5 | | OVERALL 4.25 / 5 | ★★★★☆ |

MON-FRI.	7:30am - 5:30pm
SAT-SUN.	8:30am - 5:30pm

First opened 2016
Roaster Ozone Coffee Roasters
Machine La Marzocco Linea AV, 2 groups
Grinder Mazzer Major

Espresso	£1.80
Cappuccino	£2.50
Latte	£2.50
Flat white	£2.50

www.cayaclub.com
⊖ Brixton

F.Mondays

112a Brixton Hill, SW2 1AH

F.Mondays is a small place, but it has a good choice of seating options including a counter in the window, a few individual tables, and a larger table where 'a good cross-section of the community' gathers round to work, talk, and eat. They come for excellent Alchemy espresso-based brews, and for great-looking food that includes wickedly indulgent cakes. But the best thing here is the exceptionally attractive garden in back, a hidden haven that will make you forget that the Brixton Hill traffic is just a stone's throw away.

www.fmondayscoffee.com

⊖ Brixton

| MON-FRI. | 7:00am – 4:00pm |
| SAT-SUN. | 8:00am – 5:00pm |

First opened 2014
Roaster Alchemy Coffee Roasters
Machine La Marzocco Linea, 2 groups
Grinder Anfim Scody

Espresso	£1.90
Cappuccino	£2.60
Latte	£2.60
Flat white	£2.50

MAP REF. 213

COFFEE 4.00 / 5   **OVERALL** 4.25 / 5

Federation Coffee

Unit 77-78 Brixton Village Market, Coldharbour Lane, SW9 8PS

Federation has led a flourishing of foodie culture in the rapidly developing Brixton Village Market, and is surrounded by a host of other cafés and restaurants following its lead. The seating arrayed around the outside of the café affords a prime position to people-watch and soak up the lively atmosphere of the covered market. Now under the management of Joe Cannon and Nick Balfe (owners of the highly regarded Salon restaurant), Federation offers a small but high-quality food menu and has a brew bar serving filter coffee with beans from a changing roster of guest roasters.

www.federationcoffee.com
⊖ Brixton

Sister locations Brighton Terrace Takeaway Hatch

MON-FRI.	8:00am - 5:00pm
SAT.	9:00am - 6:00pm
SUN.	9:00am - 5:00pm

First opened 2010
Roaster Curve and guests
Machine La Marzocco Linea PB, 3 groups
Grinder Nuova Simonelli Mythos One, Mahlkönig EK 43

Espresso	£2.10
Cappuccino	£2.70
Latte	£2.70
Flat white	£2.70

MAP REF. 214

COFFEE 4.50 / 5		OVERALL 4.50 / 5	

231

Flotsam & Jetsam

4 Bellevue Parade, SW17 7EQ

Proving once again that beginners can do great things in the world of coffee. Kiwi-born Hana McEwan - who had never worked in the business before, has created a first-rate local hangout. The nautical theme in the décor is handled subtly, so it looks 'like a beach house' but doesn't ride the theme too hard. There's a highly accomplished kitchen (weekend brunch is mega-popular) and an equally skilful team working with the Allpress beans. McEwan says, 'We wanted to welcome everyone.' And the locals appreciate it. Great place after a walk on the Common.

+44(0)20 8672 7639
www.flotsamandjetsamcafe.co.uk
⬤ Wandsworth Common

MON-SUN. 8:00am - 5:00pm

First opened 2015
Roaster Allpress Coffee Roasters
Machine La Marzocco Linea PB, 3 groups
Grinder Mazzer Super Jolly, Mazzer Robur

Espresso	£2.00	
Cappuccino	£2.50 / £2.80	
Latte	£2.50 / £2.80	
Flat white	£2.40 / £2.70	

MAP REF. **215**

COFFEE 4.25 / 5	🫘🫘🫘🫘◖	OVERALL 4.25 / 5	★★★★⯪

Ground Coffee Society

79 Lower Richmond Road, SW15 1ET

This star of the Putney coffee scene puts Ground Coffee Society's own beans to excellent use in both a three-group La Marzocco Strada and in batch brews. The menu is short but pushes all the right buttons for brunch and lunch, and baked goods are taken very seriously - check out the cake offering, whatever it happens to be when you visit. They also sell loose-leaf tea or smoothies if that's more to your liking - which of course it shouldn't be. In fine weather, be sure to grab a seat outside.

+44(0)20 8789 5101
www.groundcoffeesociety.com
⊖ Putney Bridge / ⇌ Putney Rail

MON-FRI.	7:00am - 6:00pm
SAT-SUN.	8:00am - 6:00pm

First opened 2010
Roaster Ground Coffee Society Roasters
Machine La Marzocco Strada, 3 groups
Grinder Mazzer Robur E x2

Espresso	£1.80
Cappuccino	£2.30 / £2.70
Latte	£2.30 / £2.70
Flat white	£2.30 / £2.70

MAP REF. **216**

COFFEE 4.50 / 5

OVERALL 4.25 / 5 ★★★★½

La Moka

179 Battersea High Street, SW11 3JS

La Moka recently moved to a bigger location and is equally irresistible. It's the sort of café you feel you ought to tell your friends about, but decide not to so you can have it all to yourself. Owners Ni and Ettore Moraschinelli have created a lovely space to enjoy a spot of breakfast or lunch. Ni, a pastry chef by training, sources a delectable selection of cakes, pastries and breads. Every aspect of the café is beautifully visualised courtesy of Ettore's graphic design skills.

+44(0)7824 669 482
www.lamoka.co.uk
⊖ Clapham Junction

MON–FRI.   7:00am – 4:00pm
SAT–SUN.   8:30am – 5:30pm

First opened 2014
Roaster Allpress Espresso
Machine La Marzocco FB/80, 2 groups
Grinder Mazzer Robur, Mazzer Super Jolly

Espresso   £2.00
Cappuccino   £2.50 / £2.70
Latte   £2.50 / £2.70
Flat white   £2.50

MAP REF.

COFFEE
4.25 / 5   🌰🌰🌰🌰🌰

OVERALL
4.25 / 5   ★★★★⯪

The Lido Cafe

Brockwell Lido, Dulwich Road, SE24 0PA

A bracing dip in Brockwell Lido is guaranteed to wake you up in the morning just as effectively as a double espresso. Happily, you don't need to take the plunge to enjoy the hospitality at The Lido Cafe. In summer, the palm-shaded terrace overlooking the pool is a special spot to sip flat whites, or even indulge in a Prosecco brunch. Open for breakfast, lunch or dinner all year round, this Art Deco retreat is a unique addition to London's café culture.

+44(0)20 7737 8183
www.thelidocafe.co.uk
⇝ Herne Hill Rail

MON-SUN. 9:00am - 5:00pm

First opened 2009
Roaster Allpress Espresso
Machine La Marzocco FB/80, 3 groups
Grinder Mazzer Robur

Espresso	£1.90
Cappuccino	£2.75
Latte	£2.75
Flat white	£2.60

MAP REF. **218**

COFFEE 4.25 / 5		OVERALL 4.25 / 5	★★★★⯪

Milk

20 Bedford Hill, SW12 9RG

Milk is a magnificent medley of artisan coffee and Aussie-style food, with a sprinkling of British eccentricity. The playful and nostalgic theme borders on the bizarre with the café's baby head motif. The hip team take their espresso very seriously, squeezing every drop of performance from their Kees van der Westen. Alternatively, try an AeroPress to appreciate the subtleties of the single origins on offer. Cupping classes are also available for those interested in developing their own coffee expertise.

+44(0)20 8772 9085
www.milk.london
⊖ Balham

MON-SAT. 8:00am - 5:00pm
SUN. 9:00am - 5:00pm

First opened 2012
Roaster The Barn, Koppi
Machine Kees van der Westen Spirit
Grinder Mahlkönig EK 43

Espresso	£2.00
Cappuccino	£2.50
Latte	£2.50
Flat white	£2.50

MAP REF. **219**

COFFEE 4.50 / 5		OVERALL 4.25 / 5	★★★★⯪

Saucer & Cup

159 Arthur Road, SW19 8AD

Saucer and Cup is small in size - tiny really, with seating for just a dozen customers. But it aims for huge quality in everything it does. Beans come from Caravan and you can have them from the La Marzocco or as filters from V60 or AeroPress. The counter is loaded throughout the day with great-looking food - everything from sandwiches and salads through indulgent cakes and small bakes. Saucer and Cup lies just outside Wimbledon Park station but it's more than just a pitstop before the morning commute.

www.saucerandcup.com
 Wimbledon Park

MON–FRI.	7:30am – 6:30pm
SAT.	8:30am – 6:30pm
SUN.	9:00am – 5:00pm

Roaster Caravan Coffee Roasters
Machine La Marzocco
Grinder Mahlkönig Peak

Espresso	£2.00
Cappuccino	£2.60
Latte	£2.60
Flat white	£2.60

MAP REF. 220

COFFEE 4.25 / 5   OVERALL 4.00 / 5 ★★★★☆

Social Pantry Café

170A Lavender Hill, SW11 5TG

This Lavender Hill café is part of a catering company, which helps to explain the emphasis on beautiful presentation. But it's not all about good looks - even though everything here, from the food through the plates to the décor, is designed to be easy on the eye. It's about quality, in the goods arrayed on the counter: light bites, filling brunches, lovely cakes and biscuits, and sandwiches featuring bacon and sausage from the Ginger Pig butcher group. They also do delivery and a picnic hamper for two, and coffee comes from Horsham Roasters.

socialpantry.co.uk
⊖ Clapham Junction

MON-WED.	7:30am - 4:00pm
THU-FRI.	7:30am - 5:00pm
SAT.	8:30am - 4:00pm
SUN.	9:00am - 4:00pm

First opened 2013
Roaster Horsham Roasters
Machine Wega EVD2, 2 groups
Grinder Mazzer

Espresso	£2.20
Cappuccino	£2.50
Latte	£2.50
Flat white	£2.50

MAP REF. 221

Stir Coffee

111 Brixton Hill, SW2 1AA

There are plenty of coffee houses that do what Stir does - simple food, casual vibe, community feeling. But few do everything as successfully as this 2016 newcomer to the Brixton scene. It's set on a corner site with big windows, so the front room gets lots of light and has good views. The back room is the preferred option if you want to escape from the outside world.

The front room is where food and coffee are served, and it's impossible not to notice the mouth-watering array of sandwiches (bagels are a speciality), which at lunchtime can be found towering over the counter. Some of the sandwiches are so deeply filled that you might need crocodile-size jaws to get your teeth

around them. Don't let them distract you from the baked goods, another impressive display. Or from the coffee, which is made with care using Mission beans and some guests. Order a latte and you may get some breath-taking latte art, so lovely you won't want to drink it.

The combination of exactly-right offerings has made Stir a favoured destination for locals, who pile in to work, chat, or commune with their kiddies - or settle in with a thriller or magazine borrowed from the bookshelf near the front door. Friendly and eager service completes the picture at this well-nigh perfect local.

MAP REF.

COFFEE 4.25 / 5

OVERALL 4.25 / 5 ★★★★☆

MON-FRI.	7:00am - 7:00pm	
SAT-SUN.	8:00am - 7:00pm	

First opened 2016
Roaster Mission Coffee Works and guests
Machine La Marzocco GB/5, 2 groups
Grinder Mazzer Super Jolly,
Mahlkönig EK 43

Espresso	£2.20
Cappuccino	£2.70
Latte	£2.50
Flat white	£2.50

+44(0)20 8333 1203
www.stircoffee.co.uk
⊖ Brixton

Story Coffee

115 St John's Hill, SW11 1SZ

Story Coffee rather belongs to a different world. A world where a person's golden time isn't bullied by smartphones, menial tasks, or wailing offspring. A world where delicious things are handed to them across the counter. A world where a beautifully-poured coffee has the power to unscramble the scrambled. Floods of light, blonde wood, fresh flowers on the tables, charming owners and an impeccable list of suppliers: it's all there. Like a great novel, Story transports you to an altogether better place.

www.storycoffee.co.uk

Clapham Junction

MON-FRI.	7:00am - 4:00pm
SAT.	8:00am - 5:00pm
SUN.	9:00am - 5:00pm

First opened 2014
Roaster Square Mile Coffee Roasters and guests
Machine Kees van der Westen Spirit, 2 groups
Grinder Nuova Simonelli Mythos, Mahlkönig EK 43

Espresso	£2.20
Cappuccino	£2.80
Latte	£2.80
Flat white	£2.80

MAP REF. 223

COFFEE 4.50 / 5

OVERALL 4.50 / 5 ★★★★⯪

Tamp Coffee

1 Devonshire Road, W4 2EU

Nestled between the chichi boutiques of Devonshire Road, Tamp resembles a rustic lodge with its wood-clad floor, ceiling, and bar. The owner's dog, ensconced in its bed at the rear of the store, completes the homely scene. This isn't just a destination to put your feet up, though. Tamp offers coffee from Bristol-based Extract Coffee Roasters and guest beans from respected international roasters including Berlin's The Barn. Even the non-homogenised milk has been carefully sourced from West Sussex's Goodwood Estate, making deliciously sweet and creamy cappuccinos.

www.tampcoffee.co.uk
⊖ Turnham Green

MON–WED.	8:00am – 5:30pm
THU–SAT.	8:00am – 6:00pm
SUN.	8:30am – 6:00pm

First opened 2014
Roaster Extract Coffee Roasters
Machine La Marzocco Linea PB
Grinder Nuova Simonelli Mythos, Anfim Drogheria, Sanremo SR70 EVO

Espresso	£2.20
Cappuccino	£2.80 / £3.25
Latte	£2.80 / £3.25

MAP REF.

COFFEE
4.25 / 5

OVERALL
4.25 / 5 ★★★★⯪

Tried & True

279 Upper Richmond Road, SW15 6SP

Tried & True brings the best of Kiwi café culture to suburban Putney. The vibe is relaxed and welcoming. The interior eschews voguish shabby chic in favour of a bright, clean, and refreshingly modern aesthetic. Square Mile espresso and single-estate filter coffees complement an award-winning brunch menu featuring homemade granola, pancakes, organic eggs, and the popular BBQ pulled pork Benedict. Friendly table service ensures a relaxing visit and a beautiful garden beckons in the summer months. Tried & True is one of a rare breed of top-class neighbourhood cafés.

+44(0)20 8789 0410
www.triedandtruecafe.co.uk
≥ Putney Rail

MON-FRI. 8:00am – 4:00pm
SAT-SUN. 8:30am – 4:30pm

First opened 2012
Roaster Square Mile Coffee Roasters
Machine La Marzocco FB/80, 3 groups
Grinder Mazzer Robur E, Mazzer Super Jolly

Espresso	£2.20
Cappuccino	£2.80
Latte	£3.00
Flat white	£2.80

MAP REF.

COFFEE
4.25 / 5

OVERALL
4.25 / 5 ★★★★⯪

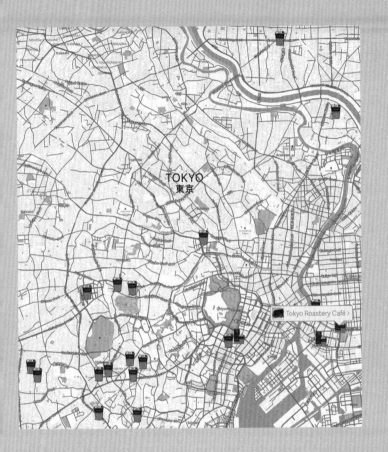

Tokyo Roastery Café ›

You'll be surprised where you can find an Allpress coffee
Download the Allpress Café Finder App to discover where

Image: Gavin Gough, Splash International.

UK COFFEE WEEK

PROJECT WATER FALL

GREAT COFFEE, GOODWILL.

663 MILLION PEOPLE AROUND THE WORLD LIVE WITHOUT A SAFE SOURCE OF WATER. UK COFFEE WEEK SUPPORTS PROJECT WATERFALL TO MAKE A DIFFERENCE IN COFFEE GROWING COMMUNITIES.

UK COFFEE WEEK SPONSORS:

HEADLINE SPONSOR

CAKESMITHS   LAVAZZA   MONIN   Arla ORGANIC Farm Milk

Home to some of London's wealthiest residents, world-renowned museums and lavish department stores, West London has a well established café culture. The number of quality-focussed coffee bars has grown in recent months, but still has a long way to go to match other London neighbourhoods.

West

A Wanted Man

330 King's Road, SW3 5UR

This is a pleasant curiosity, the first UK branch of a Singapore-based roaster and café operator (and numerous other non-coffee-related retail businesses). It has a Wild West theme, with wanted posters and such-like. If that strikes you as a strange idea for deepest Chelsea, don't let it deter you. This is a well-run, welcoming place. The high espresso roast is best suited to milky treatments, and the short menu has some imaginative dishes. Upstairs there is a beauty salon specialising in eyebrows and waxing. Further branches are planned.

+44(0)20 7351 5166
www.awantedman.co.uk
Sloane Square

MON-SUN. 8:00am - 7:00pm

First opened 2016
Roaster Common Man Coffee Roasters
Machine Synesso Cyncra, 2 groups
Grinder Nuova Simonelli Mythos One, Mahlkönig EK 43

Espresso	£2.20
Cappuccino	£2.80
Latte	£2.80
Flat white	£2.80

MAP REF. 226

  COFFEE 4.25 / 5 **OVERALL** 3.75 / 5

Antipode

28 Fulham Palace Road, W6 9PH

Australians may have afflicted us with Vegemite and Mel Gibson, but when it comes to coffee and brunch, we must concede they have something to be proud of. Antipode embodies the Australian café culture Londoners have grown to adore: velvety 'flatties', delicious smashed avocado on sourdough, and disarmingly casual service. In the evening Antipode whips out a selection of Australian craft beers and wines, with negronis thrown in for good measure. Despite hunkering in the shadow of the Hammersmith flyover, hang out here and you could just as easily be in sunny Melbourne.

+44(0)20 8741 7525
⊖ Hammersmith

MON-WED.	7:00am – 6:00pm
THU.	7:00am – 9:00pm
FRI.	7:00am – 10:00pm
SAT.	8:00am – 10:00pm
SUN.	9:00am – 4:00pm

First opened 2014
Roaster Square Mile Coffee Roasters
Machine La Marzocco Linea PB, 3 groups, Synesso Cyncra, 3 groups
Grinder Nuova Simonelli Mythos One, Mahlkönig EK 43

Espresso	£2.00
Cappuccino	£2.90 / £3.30
Latte	£2.90 / £3.30
Flat white	£2.90 / £3.30

MAP REF. 227

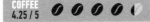

COFFEE 4.25 / 5

OVERALL 4.25 / 5 ★★★★☆

247

Artisan Ealing

32 New Broadway, Ealing, W5 2XA

TOP
35

West

Most coffee entrepreneurs would be content with several successful coffee shops. Not Artisan founders, Edwin and Magda Harrison. Not only do they have a string of sites, they also have an impressive coffee school. Connected to the main café space, the school runs home brewing masterclasses and professional SCAE-accredited qualifications. The Artisan team's enthusiasm is infectious; baristas and trainers alike are eager to surprise customers with superb guest coffees and constantly challenge themselves to push the quality bar in pursuit of coffee excellence.

+44(0)20 7998 3450
www.artisancoffee.co.uk
⊖ Ealing Broadway

Sister locations Putney / Stamford Brook / East Sheen

MON–FRI.	7:30am – 5:30pm
SAT.	8:30am – 5:30pm
SUN.	9:00am – 5:30pm

First opened 2014
Roaster Allpress Espresso, The Barn
Machine La Marzocco FB/80, 3 groups
Grinder Nuova Simonelli Mythos One

Espresso	£2.20
Cappuccino	£2.60 / £2.90
Latte	£2.60 / £2.90
Flat white	£2.60 / £2.90

MAP REF. 228

 COFFEE 4.75 / 5

OVERALL 4.50 / 5 ★★★★½

Artisan Stamford Brook

372 King Street, W6 0RX

Owners Edwin and Magda's passion for coffee began with spending time in Uganda, where they contributed to development work with coffee farmers. Artisan's London cafés do justice to the work of growers and roasters by diligently extracting great quality from top-notch beans. The interior's electric blue walls contrast magnificently with the copper counter and stools, creating a striking environment in which to enjoy the finished product. Upholding their reputation for coffee excellence, the team runs coffee brewing masterclasses for customers at their Ealing branch.

+44(0)20 3302 1434
www.artisancoffee.co.uk
⊖ Stamford Brook

MON–FRI.	7:00am – 6:00pm
SAT.	8:00am – 6:00pm
SUN.	8:30am – 6:00pm

First opened 2013
Roaster Allpress Espresso, The Barn
Machine La Marzocco FB/80, 3 groups
Grinder Nuova Simonelli Mythos One

Espresso	£2.20
Cappuccino	£2.60 / £2.90
Latte	£2.60 / £2.90
Flat white	£2.60 / £2.90

Sister locations Ealing / Putney / East Sheen

MAP REF. **229**

COFFEE 4.50 / 5   **OVERALL** 4.50 / 5   ★★★★½

Beany Green

Unit 6C, Sheldon Square, W2 6EZ

The area north of Paddington station may not abound in charm, but Beany Green creates its own. From the slightly wacky décor down to the smiling service and self-indulgent baked goods, this place is just a joy. The food centres on wraps and salads with an Australian-style emphasis on healthy eating – and in quality it is several notches above the London coffee-shop average. Espresso drinks using beans from The Roasting Party have a sweetly rounded character. Here and at its other locations, Beany Green leaves the competition looking green with envy.

+44(0)20 7289 3344
www.daisygreenfood.com
⊖ Paddington

MON-FRI.	7:30am – 5:30pm
SAT-SUN.	9:00am – 5:00pm

First opened 2014
Roaster The Roasting Party
Machine La Marzocco Linea, 3 groups
Grinder La Marzocco Vulcano

Espresso	£2.20
Cappuccino	£2.60
Latte	£2.60
Flat white	£2.60

Sister locations Broadgate / Broadgate Circle / Little Venice / Regent's Place / Portman Village / Royal Festival Hall / Victoria

MAP REF. 230

COFFEE
4.25 / 5

OVERALL
4.25 / 5 ★★★★⯪

Bluebelles

320 Portobello Road, W10 5RU

NEW

Bluebelles has been in W10 since 2012 and has built up a dedicated local following for its warm welcome, soul-satisfying brunch dishes, and outstanding coffee. But it never rests on its laurels, always looking for ways to raise its game, even changing coffee suppliers late in 2016 to get its own espresso blend from Campbell & Syme. The display of baked goods is dangerously enticing, and the gluten-free range is ever-expanding. Even in an area with no shortage of cafés, Bluebelles is a standout.

+44(0)20 8968 4572
⊖ Ladbroke Grove

Sister locations Bluebelles Mill Hill

MON-SUN.   8:00am - 4:30pm

First opened 2012
Roaster Campbell & Syme
Machine La Marzocco Linea, 2 groups
Grinder Mazzer Robur

Espresso	£2.00
Cappuccino	£2.50
Latte	£2.50
Flat white	£2.50

MAP REF. **231**

 COFFEE 4.00 / 5 **OVERALL** 4.00 / 5 ★ ★ ★ ★ ☆

251

Cable Co.

4 Bridge House, Chamberlayne Road, NW10 3NR

After years in the coffee wilderness, Kensal Rise finally has speciality coffee courtesy of Cable Co. The spartan interior of this unassuming coffee bar follows a factory theme: concrete, raw timber, and black tiling contrast with copper lamp shades which provide welcome flashes of colour. An oil drum repurposed as a sugar station completes the industrial atmosphere. Aromatic Climpson & Sons coffee is complemented by a small selection of toasties and a tempting range of cakes, including an irresistible blueberry crumble loaf cake.

+44(0)7733 341 179

⊖ Kensal Rise

Sister locations Wired Co.

| MON–FRI. | 7:30am – 5:00pm |
| SAT–SUN. | 9:00am – 5:00pm |

First opened 2014
Roaster Climpson & Sons and guests
Machine La Marzocco Linea PB, 3 Groups
Grinder Nuova Simonelli Mythos One, Mazzer Major E, Mahlkönig Tanzania

Espresso	£2.10
Cappuccino	£2.70
Latte	£2.70
Flat white	£2.60

MAP REF. **232**

COFFEE 4.25 / 5

OVERALL 4.25 / 5 ★★★★⯪

Chairs and Coffee

512 Fulham Road, SW6 5NJ

Chairs and Coffee is the labour of two friends, Simone Guerini Rocco and Roberto D'alessandro. The duo's passion emanates from every facet of the café: their Italian pride pours from the vintage Faema espresso machine (rescued from a priest's basement). Their ingenuity whirrs in the restored 1950s roaster, and the chairs casually suspended from the ceiling (because they like 'being ridiculous') embody their unbridled eccentricity. Truly authentic cafés like Chairs and Coffee are a rarity; this is one to be cherished.

+44(0)20 7018 1913
www.chairsandcoffee.co.uk
⊖ Fulham Broadway

| MON–FRI. | 8:00am – 6:00pm |
| SAT–SUN. | 9:00am – 6:00pm |

First opened 2013
Roaster 80 Stone Coffee Roasters
Machine Faema E61, 2 groups
Grinder Mazzer Major x2, Mahlkönig EK 43

Espresso	£1.80 / £2.00
Cappuccino	£2.50
Latte	£2.50
Flat white	£2.50

MAP REF. **233**

COFFEE 4.25 / 5

OVERALL 4.25 / 5 ★★★★⯪

Chief Coffee

Turnham Green Terrace Mews, W4 1QU

NEW

Located in a mews around the corner from Turnham Green station, Chief Coffee occupies a building that began life as a Victorian bottling factory. Their regular beans come from Workshop and Allpress, but there might also be a guest pour-over from the excellent Barn roaster in Berlin. You can have a light lunch, a cake or one of their brownies. And if you're feeling nimble-fingered, they have a pinball lounge with nine machines. Seriously consider one of those pour-overs. But if you order, ask for a swan on top.

www.chief-coffee.com
⊖ Turnham Green

MON-FRI.	8:00am - 5:30pm
SAT.	9:00am - 6:00pm
SUN.	10:00am - 5:30pm

First opened 2015
Roaster Allpress Espresso, Workshop Coffee and guests
Machine La Marzocco FB/80
Grinder Mahlkönig EK 43, Mazzer Kony

Espresso	£2.00
Cappuccino	£2.40
Latte	£2.40
Flat white	£2.40

MAP REF. 234

Coffee Geek and Friends

Unit 22 Cardinal Place, 6 Cathedral Walk, SW1E 5JH

The new developments around Victoria Station are not exactly big on warmth, but Coffee Geek lives up to the second part of its name: this is a really friendly place. It's a great spot for enjoying lunch, baked goods, or just a beautifully brewed coffee. Two espresso machines (total of five groups) are needed to cope with peak times, and three chefs make most of their baked goods on the premises, a rarity in a place this size. While you're there, be sure to check out the incredibly clever water filtration system.

+44(0)20 3417 3600
www.coffeegeekandfriends.co.uk
🚇 Victoria

MON-FRI.	7:00am – 5:00pm
SAT.	9:00am – 5:00pm
SUN.	9:00am – 3:00pm

First opened 2015
Roaster Allpress Espresso
Machine La Marzocco Linea PB, 3 groups, La Marzocco Linea PB, 2 groups
Grinder Nuova Simonelli Mythos One, Mazzer Kold

Espresso	£1.80
Cappuccino	£2.60
Latte	£2.60
Flat white	£2.60

MAP REF. 235

| COFFEE 4.25 / 5 | OVERALL 4.25 / 5 |

Electric Coffee Co.

40 Haven Green, W5 2NX

Stepping inside this Ealing enclave, one's gaze is immediately stolen by the Kees van der Westen Mirage coffee machine. Crafted with aircraft-grade aluminium, this stunning machine is the supercharged dynamo of Electric Coffee Co. Piloted by an enthusiastic team, the Mirage fires out gutsy house-roasted espresso. Filter coffee is also available should you prefer a more gentle take-off. Electric Coffee Co. is one of the best third wave coffee shops in the west.

+44(0)20 8991 1010
www.electriccoffee.co.uk
⊖ Ealing Broadway

MON-FRI.	7:00am - 6:00pm
SAT.	8:00am - 6:00pm
SUN.	9:00am - 6:00pm

First opened 2008
Roaster Electric Coffee Co. Roasters / Electric Blend
Machine Kees van der Westen Mirage Veloce, 3 groups
Grinder Mazzer Robur E x2, Anfim Super Caimano

Espresso	£2.10
Cappuccino	£2.70 / £2.90
Latte	£2.70 / £2.90
Flat white	£2.70

MAP REF. 236

COFFEE 4.50 / 5   **OVERALL** 4.50 / 5 ★★★★⯪

The Elgin

255 Elgin Avenue, W9 1NJ

The three-group La Marzocco gets a good workout when The Elgin is busy. And it's busy a lot, even during the week, when local kids (and their parents) congregate for food and drinks. The ground-floor café/bar/restaurant was originally an old-fashioned pub and takes advantage of that expansive space, now decorated in a combination of traditional and industrial. Attention to detail shows in the piping-hot cup that held a bracing shot of Coleman coffee. Food is serious, changing three times a day and combining modern British with a good dose of Italian and Spanish flair.

+44(0)20 7625 5511
theelgin.com
⊖ Maida Vale

MON-THU.	8:00am - 11:00pm
FRI.	8:00am - 12:00am
SAT.	9:00am - 12:00am
SUN.	9:30am - 10:30pm

First opened 2013
Roaster Coleman Coffee
Machine La Marzocco Linea, 3 groups
Grinder Mazzer x3

Espresso	£2.40 / £2.80
Cappuccino	£2.80
Latte	£2.80
Flat white	£2.80

MAP REF. 237

COFFEE 4.25 / 5   **OVERALL** 4.25 / 5 ★★★★⯪

Farm Girl

59a Portobello Road, W11 3DB

When Farm Girl first appeared in 2015, at the Notting Hill end of Portobello Road, it quickly became apparent that this was the right place opening at the right time. This Australian outpost of virtuous eating has become a major destination, and it's not just because of visitors hitting the antique markets (though Saturday lunch will guarantee a long queue). People come here because the food's great, and the coffee too. Its emphasis on healthy living is so hard-core Notting Hill that they cook their omelettes in coconut oil, and don't even offer full-fat milk in their coffees.

But semi-skimmed doesn't equate to semi-good. There's close attention to detail in every aspect of the food and drink, from their own granola blend through well assembled, carefully dressed salads and imaginative sandwiches. Tea drinks, juices and flavoured waters complete the healthy picture on the drinks list. The coffee comes from The Roasting Party in Winchester, and the baristas know everything about how to brew it and make it look beautiful. Sit in the pretty little courtyard if the weather allows. If not, the colourful interior, with a big wall-hung basket of fresh fruit and lively paintings, is a treat for the eyes.

MAP REF.

COFFEE 4.25 / 5	OVERALL 4.50 / 5

West

MON-SAT.	8:30am - 4:30pm
SUN.	9:00am - 4:00pm

First opened 2015
Roaster The Roasting Party
Machine La Marzocco Linea AV, 3 groups
Grinder Mazzer Robur E

Espresso	£2.20
Cappuccino	£2.80
Latte	£2.80
Flat white	£2.80

+44(0)20 7229 4678
www.thefarmgirl.co.uk
 Notting Hill

Fernandez & Wells South Kensington

8a Exhibition Road, SW7 2HF

This Fernandez & Wells' venue is a godsend for coffee-starved West Londoners and visitors to the nearby museums. The interior's high ceiling and elegant cornicing resonate with South Kensington's noble architecture. Cured meats hang artfully against the rear wall, accompanied by a shelf of well-chosen wines. There's plenty of seating round the back, which is fortunate as you'll almost certainly want to complement your Has Bean coffee with a plate of charcuterie.

+44(0)20 7589 7473
www.fernandezandwells.com
⊖ South Kensington

Sister locations Denmark Street / Duke Street / Lexington Street / Somerset House

| MON-SAT. | 8:00am - 11:00pm |
| SUN. | 8:00am - 8:00pm |

First opened 2012
Roaster Has Bean bespoke blend
Machine La Marzocco Linea PB, 3 groups
Grinder Nuova Simonelli Mythos One

Espresso	£2.60
Cappuccino	£2.95
Latte	£2.95
Flat white	£2.95

MAP REF. 239

Granger & Co Notting Hill

175 Westbourne Grove, W11 2SB

 NEW

Bill Granger's Australia-style approach to eating and drinking makes a perfect fit with this posh patch of Notting Hill, who have taken to it enthusiastically. The downside is that if you show up without a booking at mealtimes, you'd better resign yourself to waiting. This is smaller than their other two sites, and even on a cold day there may well be a queue. But it's a pleasure to come outside peak mealtimes for a cookie or piece of fudge, washed down with well-made milky drinks or (our favourite) their cold drip coffee.

+44(0)20 7229 9111
grangerandco.com
⊖ Notting Hill Gate

| MON-SAT. | 7:00am - 11:00pm |
| SUN. | 8:00am - 10:30pm |

   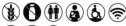

First opened 2011
Roaster Allpress Espresso
Machine La Marzocco Linea AV, 3 groups
Grinder Mazzer Robur, Mazzer Super Jolly

Espresso	£2.80
Cappuccino	£2.80
Latte	£2.80
Flat white	£2.80

Sister locations Clerkenwell / King's Cross

MAP REF. 240

Hally's

60 New Kings Road, SW6 4LS

The vibe at Hally's is airy California cool. The reclaimed clapboard and whitewashed brick walls are punctuated by citrus yellow bar stools and neon signs. You may just be popping in for a Monmouth coffee, but be prepared to stay for longer once you catch sight of the food on offer, which includes an outstanding array of salads and a bold-flavoured brunch menu. Across the street, sister shop Little H offers a condensed Hally's menu including breakfast, lunch and fabulous fresh juices and smoothies.

+44(0)20 3302 7408
www.hallyslondon.com
⊖ Parsons Green

Sister locations Little H

MON–SUN. 8:00am – 6:00pm

First opened 2013
Roaster Monmouth Coffee Company
Machine La Marzocco Linea, 2 groups
Grinder Mazzer Kold

Espresso	£2.00
Cappuccino	£2.70 / £3.00
Latte	£2.70 / £3.00
Flat white	£2.70 / £3.00

MAP REF. **241**

COFFEE
4.25 / 5

OVERALL
4.50 / 5 ★★★★⯨

Halva

771 Fulham Road, SW6 5HA

'Halva' means sweet, and the word couldn't be more appropriate for this delightful bakery/café. Small and simply decorated, it caters for an international clientele with baked goods based in the rigorous French training of the owner. Coffee comes from The Roastery, and the espresso cups some very lively berry flavours. But the undisputed star draw here is the baking, whether it's rich quiche in a feather-light pastry, Paris-perfect croissants, or a loaf of outstanding French-style sourdough to take home. This part of Fulham has a village-y feel, and it's not surprising that many customers are regulars.

+44(0)20 7384 2045
halvabakery.co.uk
Parsons Green

MON–FRI.	7:30am – 7:00pm
SAT.	8:00am – 6:00pm
SUN.	8:00am – 2:00pm

First opened 2015
Roaster The Roastery
Machine La Marzocco Linea, 2 groups
Grinder Mazzer Major E

Espresso	£1.70 / £1.90
Cappuccino	£2.50 / £2.70
Latte	£2.50 / £2.70
Flat white	£2.70

MAP REF. 242

| COFFEE 4.00 / 5 | | OVERALL 4.25 / 5 | ★★★★⯪ |

Iris & June

1 Howick Place, SW1P 1WG

The arrival of Iris & June (named after the owner's grandparents) marked a turning point in the fortunes for the neighbourhood. The interior's concrete floors, exposed ventilation ducts, and industrial tiling lend the café an air of Shoreditch cool. Upon entering, customers are greeted by a sumptuous display of salads and sandwiches behind polished glass. Iris & June feels like a keystone in the new Victoria, injecting a dose of vigour and setting a high standard for a stylish, intelligent coffee bar in an area previously bereft of speciality coffee.

+44(0)20 7828 3130
www.irisandjune.com
Victoria / St James's Park

| MON–FRI. | 7:30am – 5:30pm |
| SAT–SUN. | 9:00am – 4:00pm |

First opened 2014
Roaster Ozone Coffee Roasters and guests
Machine La Marzocco Strada, 3 groups
Grinder Mazzer Luigi, Mahlkönig EK 43

Espresso	£2.50
Cappuccino	£2.90
Latte	£2.90
Flat white	£2.90

MAP REF. 243

| COFFEE 4.50 / 5 |  | OVERALL 4.50 / 5 | ★★★★⯪ |

St Clements Cafe

201 New Kings Road, SW6 4SR

The menu at St Clements is so good it presents some tough decisions. Agonising choices must be made between seductive salads and tantalising tarts. Olivia Cundy, a professional chef with ten years' experience, composes marvellous plates of seasonal fare, paired with hand-roasted coffee from Cast Iron Coffee Roasters. The café offers comfortable seating and a delightful terrace opening out to the street. Little details like bone-handled knives and tasteful teal decor lend the café an air of elegance.

+44(0)20 7998 8919
www.stclementscafe.co.uk
Parsons Green

MON-FRI.	8:00am - 5:00pm
SAT.	8:30am - 5:30pm
SUN.	9:00am - 5:30pm

First opened 2014
Roaster Cast Iron Coffee Roasters
Machine La Marzocco FB/80, 2 groups
Grinder Mazzer Kony, Mazzer Super Jolly

Espresso	£2.30
Cappuccino	£3.00
Latte	£3.00
Flat white	£2.80

MAP REF. 244

COFFEE 4.00 / 5

OVERALL 4.50 / 5 ★★★★⯪

Timmy Green

Nova Building, Bressenden Place, SW1E 5DD

The Beany Green group's newest venue is a radical departure from their other venues, a gleaming modern box set in a new building near Victoria, with huge windows and two floors. It's also much more a 'proper restaurant': if you want a cocktail or a steak, you'll find it here. But coffee remains at the centre of what they do, whether from the canary-yellow La Marzocco or filter fed by an SP9 brewer. There's a coffee truck if you want to drink your coffee elsewhere, but the fabulous space (inside or out) makes it worth perching here for a while.

+44(0)20 3019 7404
www.daisygreenfood.com
⊖ Victoria

Sister locations Broadgate / Broadgate Circle / Portman Village / Little Venice / Regents Place / Royal Festival Hall

MON–SUN. 7:00am – 12:00am

First opened 2016
Roaster The Roasting Party
Machine La Marzocco 3EE, 3 groups
Grinder DIP DK-30, Mazzer Kold E

Espresso	£2.60
Cappuccino	£3.00
Latte	£3.00
Flat white	£3.00

MAP REF. **245**

COFFEE
4.25 / 5

OVERALL
4.50 / 5 ★★★★⯨

12–15 APRIL 2018
OLD TRUMAN BREWERY, BRICK LANE.

www.londoncoffeefestival.com

Behind every cup of coffee is a unique story. On its journey from coffee tree to cup, coffee passes through the hands of a number of skilled individuals. Over the following pages, expert contributors share their specialist knowledge. As you will see, the coffee we enjoy is the result of a rich and complex process, and there is always something new to learn.

Coffee Knowledge

Coffee at Origin

by **Mike Riley**, Falcon Speciality Green Coffee Importers

If you go into London's vibrant coffee community today and ask any good barista what makes a perfect cup of coffee, they will always tell you that it starts with the bean. Beyond the roasting technique, the perfect grind, and exact temperatures and precision pressure of a modern espresso machine, we must look to the dedicated coffee farmer who toils away in the tropical lands of Africa, Asia and Latin America. They are the first heroes of our trade.

Approximately 25 million people in over 50 countries are involved in producing coffee. The bean, or seed to be exact, is extracted from cherries that most commonly ripen red but sometimes orange or yellow. The cherries are usually hand-picked then processed by various means. Sometimes they are dried in the fruit under tropical sunshine until they resemble raisins - a process known as 'natural'. The 'honey process' involves pulping the fresh cherries to extract the beans which are then sundried, still coated in their sticky mucilage. Alternatively, in the 'washed process', the freshly pulped beans are left to stand in tanks of water for several hours where enzyme activity breaks down the mucilage, before they are sundried on concrete patios or raised beds. Each method has a profound impact on the ultimate flavour of the coffee.

The term 'speciality coffee' is used to differentiate the world's best from the rest. This means it has to be Arabica, the species of coffee that is often bestowed with incredible flavours - unlike its hardy cousin Robusta which is usually reserved for commercial products and many instant blends. But being Arabica alone is by no means enough for a coffee to achieve the speciality tag, since the best beans are usually those grown at higher altitude on rich and fertile soils. As well as country and region of origin, the variety is important too; Bourbon, Typica, Caturra, Catuai, Pacamara and Geisha to name but a few. Just as Shiraz and Chardonnay grapes have their own complex flavours, the same is true of coffee's varieties. Some of the world's most amazing coffees are the result of the farmer's innovative approach to experimentation with growing and production techniques, meaning that today's speciality roaster is able to source coffees of incredible complexity and variation.

A good coffee establishment will showcase coffees when they are at their best - freshly harvested and seasonal, just like good fruit and vegetables. Seasonal espresso blends change throughout the year to reflect this.

As speciality coffee importers we source stand-out coffees by regularly travelling to origin countries. Direct trade with farmers is always our aim. Above all, we pay sustainable prices and encourage them to treat their land, and those who work it, with respect. Such an approach is increasingly demanded by London's speciality coffee community in order to safeguard the industry's future.

267

Small Batch Roasting

by **Kurt Stewart**, Roaster and Co-owner, Volcano Coffee Works

I was brought up in a household dedicated to pickling, baking, sauce making and preserving. After experimenting with home brewing and wine making, my first foray into the aromatic world of small batch roasting was inevitable.

My own first experiments in small batch roasting started at home with some green beans and a wok. Of course roasting at home is much like home cooking, but when the term is applied to a commercial enterprise, it encompasses the passion and adventure of a home cook with the control and precision of a gourmet chef.

The art behind developing and building a roasting profile for a particular coffee is approached in the same way a chef develops cuisine, or a vintner crafts a wine. Culinary rules and science apply in equal measure. The roaster builds layers of flavour, working with the ingredients, sometimes pushing or manipulating the properties of an individual bean, to achieve the desired balance of sweetness, acidity, body, and the right mouth-feel and aftertaste. Coffee and wine share a vocabulary of descriptors, but as coffee has more flavour molecules than wine, coffee descriptors reach further into the culinary world. You will hear words describing aspects of flavour and taste senses, such as fruit acidity, sweet roundness, viscous syrup body, juicy plum, creamy, buttery, velvet chocolate textures. Delicious!

When a green bean is roasted, three fundamental processes occur that impact the flavours of the bean: enzyme by-products develop (giving the floral, citrus and fruity aromas), sugars brown (giving the sweet, caramel and nutty aromas), and plant fibres in the bean are roasted, known as dry-distillation (giving the spicy and smokey flavours). Only the enzyme by-products (which come from the coffee plant itself) are due to the bean chosen for roasting, whilst the remaining two processes are the result of how the bean is roasted. This is why no two small batch roasters will create an identical flavour profile from the same bean. Like chefs, each roaster will identify with, single out and highlight a flavour or combination of flavours which pleases, satisfies or amazes their palate.

Small Batch Roasting is a term reserved for those using roasting equipment controlled by the human hand rather than computers. A skilled roaster who understands his equipment, maintains ducting, understands heat/air ratios and extraction principles, coupled with following some basic fundamentals, can draw out origin characteristics and individual nuances, and create a roast where the optimum flavour potential is realised.

The roasting equipment itself is fundamentally a steel drum, which is usually heated by a gas flame. The drum constantly revolves, and at around 10 minutes of roasting at 203-205°C the developing beans reach 'first crack' (a bit like popcorn cracking). If roasting stops here, it will be a mild or lighter roast. When roasting continues, samples are taken with every revolution of the drum and the roaster observes the developing bean's colour, mass and aroma. The roaster may apply more or less heat or air and will remove the beans once they have reached the desired roast profile. This is usually within a 20 minute roasting time and often before second crack is reached as beyond this point the beans can lose their subtle origin characteristics and begin to take on a generic burnt flavour. The beans then enter the cooling tray until cool to touch. This process is in stark contrast to the large scale computer controlled commercial roasting process that takes between 90 seconds and 10 minutes at temperatures in excess of 360 °C. The beans are then doused with water to cool them. Although this is the most economic way to roast beans, it takes away any input by the roaster and does not give the bean enough time to develop fully.

When a roastery operation gets to such a scale that the roaster becomes distanced from their beans due to mechanised roasting processes and machinery, the instinct and hands-on effect that define a small batch roaster's product will always become somewhat diminished. And therein lies the excitement and diversity that small batch roasting offers over and above large-scale operations. It comes down to the physical ability of a talented roaster to exercise his or her senses, passion, enthusiasm, and the art of roasting.

Coffee Tasting

by **Lynsey Harley**, Founder, Modern Standard Coffee

Coffee tasting is the process of identifying the characteristics of a particular coffee. In the coffee industry, professional 'cupping' sessions are conducted to evaluate coffees on a range of attributes. Cupping helps coffee buyers select which coffees to buy, and identify desirable attributes for formulating blends.

Coffee is most commonly scored using The Specialty Coffee Association of America (SCAA) system. Coffees achieving a score of 85 or higher (from a maximum of 100) are regarded as 'specialty' grade. These coffees have no defects and have a very distinct pleasant flavour profile. Coffees are scored on the following attributes: aroma, flavour, aftertaste, acidity, body, sweetness, cleanliness, uniformity and balance.

The cupping process follows a set procedure: 8.25g of coarsely ground coffee is measured into a shallow cup, specifically designed for the purpose. 150ml of water heated to 92°C is added and left for 4 minutes. Next, a spoon is used to break and remove the 'crust', which provides the first opportunity to sample the coffee's aroma. After a further 6 minutes, the cupper begins to taste the coffee. Different attributes are evaluated at intervals as the coffee cools.

70°C: Flavour and Aftertaste

Flavour: The coffee's principle flavour; what are your taste buds telling you?

Aftertaste: The length of positive flavour qualities after the coffee has been swallowed.

70°C – 60°C: Acidity and Body

Acidity: Bright for positive acidity, sour for negative. Positive acidity adds to the coffee's sweetness.

Body: The 'weight' of the brew. Is it heavy like a good red wine, or light and refined like a sauvignon blanc?

38°C: Sweetness and Cleanliness

Sweetness: Is the coffee sweet and pleasing?

Cleanliness: When no defects are found, the cup is clean.

Balance: Greater than the sum of its parts. Flavour, aftertaste, acidity and body work together to achieve balance.

One coffee can taste dramatically different depending on the processing method. Washing coffees increases the acidity, whilst the semi-washed process gives a honeyed sweetness to the coffee. The natural processing method can increase the sweetness, and can also encourage development of more obscure flavours including strawberry, blueberry and creamy notes.

Tasting coffee at home can be fun; exploring what a coffee can offer in terms of flavour, sweetness and other attributes is exciting. Your local speciality coffee shop can offer advice on which coffees are in season, and many will sell beans for you to experiment with at home. There's a coffee out there for everyone.

SCAA Coffee taster's wheel

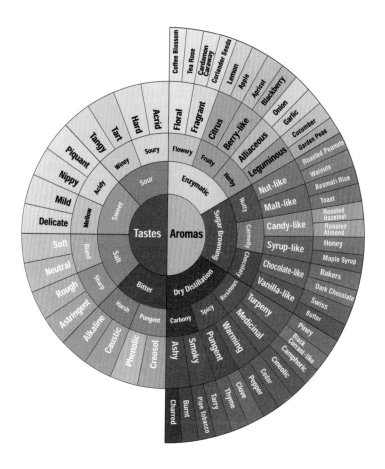

271

Coffee Grinding

by **Jeremy Challender**, Co-owner and Director of Training, Prufrock Coffee and the

Grinder technology is about to change radically. Machine design, techniques behind the bar and hand brewing methodology have improved rapidly over recent years. Manufacturers are starting to address this by seeking feedback from users as well as lab testing. Home users can benefit from these changes too. New designs entering the market have drawn directly from the experiences of barista champions. Grinder designers are seeking professional and consumer feedback on taste, flavour and ergonomics through direct collaboration and field testing. Manufacturers are aware that we need development to continue and, now more than ever, baristas have a voice in this process. To be a barista in this time of grinder development is very exciting.

With all brew methods the challenge is replicating flavour and strength. Once we've got a precise brew recipe for a coffee we stand a better chance of extracting our coffee consistently. Commercially, the easiest way to navigate from this baseline towards the optimum extraction level is with micro-adjustments in the exposed surface area of the grinds - so the grinder is key to managing flavour in the cup.

The challenge grinder designers face is how to create consistency of grind size and shape. If you get out the microscope, and a set of test sieves, you start to realise all your grinds aren't the same size, nor are they all the same shape. If they were all the same size and shape, brewing would be much easier to control. In espresso you will have seen tiny granules in your cup that are smaller than the holes in the filter basket. We call these fines. These small particles have very high surface area and extract very quickly. As a home brewer, you could consider following the example of many championship baristas; invest in laboratory test sieves to remove a portion of particles under a certain size to reduce over-extracted flavours.

There is a portion of particles that fit side-on between the burrs and are planed rather than ground. We call these larger particles boulders. They have a much lower surface area relative to their size and in a 30 second espresso extraction will under-extract. Wobbly hand grinders are real offenders in the production of boulders. These too can be sieved out.

Sharp burrs are considered to reduce fines production. Ceramic burrs, which many hand grinders are fitted with, are very durable but are often not very sharp to start with. The material of choice at the moment is titanium-coated steel. Large burr diameter is linked to lower production of fines and boulders (more 'modal' distribution) so enormous bag grinders are being examined for application in espresso making. Cutting systems like spice grinders produce a very high proportion of fines and boulders, so are not recommended.

Keeping the coffee cool during grinding is a challenge. Burrs get hot in use because of friction, and some of the most exciting developments recently have focused on temperature stability of the burrs and burr casing with the addition of heating elements and fans. A warm grinder behaves differently to a cold or a hot one, so the particle shape and size are dependent on both grind setting and temperature.

Modern grinder design is very focussed on ease of access for regular cleaning. Arabica coffee has up to 17% fat content. We only extract a small percentage of this into a beverage but even after a day of commercial use, a grinder will have a slick of fats and tiny fine particles built up around the burr casing and the barrel and throat of the grinder. Oils oxidise, so grinders must be opened up and thoroughly swept out on a regular basis. Burrs can be washed in soapy water or coffee cleaner, or abrasive oil absorbing grinder cleaning granules can be used. Home baristas have an advantage here by being able to clean after a few shots rather than after a full day's usage.

The final hurdle to overcome is grind retention: many grinders on the market have large barrels and throats that can store as much as 40g of grinds that must be squeezed out before fresh grinds appear. At Prufrock, we are moving away from grinders with a high retention of grinds as we are looking to optimise freshness. When grind changes are required we want the benefit of micro-adjustment to be immediate. Here, home baristas are also well placed, as hand grinders have zero retention of grinds and some very high quality espresso hand grinders are now available on the market.

Over the last decade we have felt that machine technology has been in advance of grinders. We often comment that a barista's top priority should be the choice of grinder. Find a great grinding solution and great coffee will follow.

Photo: Jacob Thue

Espresso

by **Ben Townsend** Trainer, London School of Coffee

The last 5 years have seen a rapid pace of development for coffee in London. The emergence of new cafés and roasteries continues apace as does the evolution of espresso technique. This "new world" culture is constantly pushing the boundaries of what is possible with the equipment, coffee and scientific knowledge that we currently have.

In a curious way, some of what is new is in fact quite old, and refers back to the largely disregarded tradition of Italian espresso. Of course, many practices remain deliberately different to traditional espresso - but it's instructive to note that the cutting edge of machine and grinder technology belongs again to the Italians, albeit achieved by recruiting non-Italian "new world" baristas to consult on the design.

Probably the most important series of changes over the last few years has been an increased understanding of grinding and extraction. Put simply, we can accurately measure with a laser refractometer how much of the desirable (or undesirable) soluble compounds in coffee have been extracted from the ground coffee by the brew water and the resulting effect on flavour.

To many people, notably espresso traditionalists, much London espresso has been unpalatably sour. We realise now that a combination of light roasting and short Antipodean style shots has been severely underextracting our coffee, producing sour brews and overly simple flavour profiles.

All of London's serious cafés are now using brew recipes. A recipe describes per shot how much ground coffee goes in, how much liquid coffee comes out and over what time duration. Apart from allowing much more consistency from shot to shot, brew recipes are typically designed to produce as much sweetness and complexity as possible, without losing too much texture. We realise now that we should have been pushing more water through our coffee to extract more solubles and reduce sourness - the Italians have been doing this for decades!

I sincerely hope that we will not see the return of stale, over-roasted or Robusta coffee made on dirty machines. Traditional goals like thick crema on an espresso are very unreliable indicators of quality. The specialty scene has its colours firmly nailed to the mast of traceable, high quality, well processed and freshly roasted beans. Balanced, clean and fresh flavours that truly reveal the character of each coffee should be the goal of both barista and consumer.

Accordingly, it appears that the next wave of machine technology has finally lost the bewildering obsession with temperature and pressure control and moved onto technology to automate the brew recipe process. In practice, this means accurately dosing grinders and new "gravimetric" machines that cut the output of the shot using beverage mass instead of water volume or time. It will not be long before the weakest link in the physical production process will be the barista - a sobering thought!

The increased understanding of brew process and its resultant focus on brew recipes and extraction yield has turned scrutiny on roast profile. Those roasters producing the most soluble coffees, without baking or over-roasting, will be favoured by the best cafés.

We have also seen the emergence of a well-informed prosumer barista. Many home setups rival that of commercial cafés, and some home baristas are more technically informed than virtually all professional baristas, via internet blogs and some excellent new books.

When asked, I still advise that espresso is a drink to be enjoyed in a communal environment. For that reason I always go out for my flat whites and espresso. Coffee is about flavour, but not just that. It's an enjoyable route to shared social experience, whether you are leaning on a marble bar in Rome or a grungy wooden counter in Hackney.

Water - The Enigma

by **Maxwell Colonna-Dashwood**, Co-owner, Colonna and Small's, UK Barista Champion 2012 & 2014

This vital ingredient is the foundation of every cup of coffee you have ever tasted, apart from the bean itself of course.

It's not just coffee that relies so dramatically on this everyday and seemingly straightforward substance. The worlds of craft beer and whisky are suitable comparisons, with breweries and distilleries proudly signifying the provenance of their water as being a vital part of their product.

A roaster, though, sells coffee, the water bit comes post sale. The water will be different and unique based on the locality of brewing, and this is on top of all of the other variables that define coffee brewing such as grinding, temperature and brew ratios. The reality is that the impact of water is rarely directly witnessed, with the other variables often being seen as the cause for dramatic flavour changes. You may be wondering right now, how big an impact can it really have?

I'm yet to present the same coffee brewed with different waters to drinkers and not have them exclaim "I can't believe how different they are, they taste like different coffees'. These aren't "coffee people" either, but customers who contested prior to the tasting that "you may be able to taste the difference but I doubt I can tell."

It may make you question whether the coffee that you tried and weren't particularly keen on, was a representative version of what the bean actually tastes like, or at the least what it is capable of tasting of like.

So, why the big difference, what is in the water?

Nearly all water that trickles out of a tap or sits in a bottle is not just water. As well as the H_2O there are other bits and bobs in the water. Minerals mainly. These have a big impact not only on what we extract from the coffee but also how that flavour sits in the cup of coffee.

It's fair to say that currently the way the coffee industry discusses water is through the use of a measurement called Total Dissolved Solids (TDS).

TDS has become the measurement which is relied upon to distinguish and inform us about how water will affect our coffee. It gives us a total of everything in the water. The problem though, is that TDS doesn't tell us everything we need to know about the water; it doesn't tell us about what those solids are. On top of this, TDS meters don't measure some non-solids that have a huge impact on flavour.

In the water, we need the minerals calcium and magnesium to help pull out a lot of the desirable flavour in the coffee, but we also need the right amount of buffering ability in the water to balance the acids. This buffering ability can be noted as the bicarbonate content of the water. So for example an "empty" soft water with no minerals will lack flavour complexity and the lack of buffer will mean a more vinegary acidity.

A good test is to make the same coffee with both Evian and Tesco Ashbeck water. Evian has a good amount of calcium and magnesium to pull flavour out, but this is accompanied by a high bicarbonate content which flattens everything out and results in a heavy, bitter and chalky brew. The Ashbeck has little extraction power so is quite empty but has a low buffer so the acidity verges on sour. For bottled waters, Waitrose Essential yields pleasant results.

However the coffee shops in this guide will most likely have a trick up their sleeve.

The industry filtration systems that have been developed primarily to stop scale build up in the striking and valuable espresso machines, also produce water compositions that are more often than not preferable for coffee brewing. Speciality coffee shops require all manner of specifics to be obsessed over and carefully executed. That cup of coffee that hits you and stops you in your step with intense, balanced and complex flavour will owe its brilliance to careful brewing, a knowledgeable brewer and superb equipment. However, it also owes a significant part of its beautiful character and flavour to the water it is brewed with.

Brewing Coffee at Home

by **Christian Baker, David Robson, Sam Mason & The London Coffee Guide**

Y ou may be surprised to know that coffee brewed at home can rival that of your favourite coffee shop. All you need is good quality ingredients and some inexpensive equipment. Keep in mind that small variations in grind coarseness, coffee /water ratio and brew time will make a significant difference to flavour, and that trial and error is the key to unlocking perfection.

Whole Beans: Whole bean coffee is superior to pre-ground. Coffee rapidly deteriorates once ground, so buy your coffee in whole bean form and store it in an air-tight container at room temperature. It should be consumed between three and thirty days after roast and ground only moments before brewing.

Water: Water is important because it makes up over 98% of the finished drink. Only use bottled water, preferably with a dry residue between 80-150mg/l. London tap water is not suitable for brewing - it will inhibit your ability to extract flavour and reveal only a fraction of a coffee's potential.

Digital scales: Get a set of scales accurate to 1g and large enough to hold your coffee brewer. Coffee is commonly measured in 'scoops' or 'tablespoons', but coffee and water are best measured by weight for greater accuracy and to ensure repeatability. Small changes in the ratio of coffee to water can have a significant impact on flavour. A good starting point is 60-70g of coffee per litre of water. Apply this ratio to meet the size of your brewer.

Grinder

A burr grinder is essential. Burr grinders are superior to blade grinders because they allow the grind coarseness to be set and produce a more consistent size of coffee fragment (critical for an even extraction). As a general rule, the coarser the grind the longer the brew time required, and vice versa. For example, an espresso needs a very fine grind whereas a French Press works with a coarser grind.

French Press

Preheat the French Press with hot water, and discard. Add 34g of coarsely ground coffee and pour in 500g of water just below boiling point (94/95°C). Steep for 4 to 5 minutes then gently plunge to the bottom. Decant the coffee straight away to avoid over-brewing (known as over-extraction).

AeroPress

The AeroPress is wonderfully versatile. It can be used with finely ground coffee and a short steep time, or with a coarser grind and a longer steep time. The latter is our preferred method for its flavour and repeatability. Preheat the AeroPress using hot water, and discard. Rinse the paper filter before securing, and place the AeroPress over a sturdy cup or jug. Add 16g of coffee and pour in 240g of water at 95°C. Secure the plunger on top, creating a seal. Steep for 3 minutes then plunge over 20 seconds.

Pour Over

We recommend using a pouring kettle for better pouring control. Place a filter paper in the cone and rinse through with hot water. Add 15g of coffee and slowly pour 30g of 95°C water to pre-soak the coffee grounds. This creates the 'bloom'. After 30 seconds add 250g of water, pouring steadily in a circular motion over the centre. It should take 1 minute and 45 seconds to pour and between 30-45 seconds to drain through. The key is to keep the flow of water steady. If the water drains too quickly/slowly, adjust the coarseness of the grind to compensate.

Stovetop

A stovetop will not make an espresso, it will, however, make a strong coffee. Pour hot water in to the base to the fill-line or just below the pressure release valve. Fill the basket with ground coffee of medium coarseness (between Pour Over and French Press). Traditional wisdom suggests a fine grind in pursuit of espresso, but stovetops extract differently to espresso machines and grinding fine is a recipe for bitter, over-extracted coffee. Screw the base to the top and place on the heat. When you hear bubbling, remove immediately and decant to ensure the brewing has stopped.

Illustrations: Zoë Barker

Traditional Pump Espresso Machine

Traditional pump espresso machines are ideal for that barista experience to create espresso-based coffee at home. Coffee should be freshly and finely ground and dosed into single or double shot filter baskets. It is then tamped to extract full flavour aroma and coffee crema. The machine controls temperature for a more consistent cup. To enjoy milk drinks such as flat whites and cappuccinos simply froth fresh milk using the steam wand (stay below 70°C) and top up your espresso.

Bean to Cup Machine

Bean to Cup provides the perfect 'coffee shop' fix and fast. It gives you all the versatility of choice and personalisation of a traditional pump machine. At the touch of a button, it burr-grinds fresh beans and froths milk (some machines even have a built in carafe), creating a fresh taste for your cup. You can personalise the strength, length, temperature, and even the froth setting. One-touch drink options make your personalised coffee time and again, without mess or fuss.

Guidelines for creating perfect latte art

by **Dhan Tamang**, UK Latte Art Champion 2013, 2014, 2015 & 2016

4 essential steps to create beautiful Latte Art.

1 Preparation

You'll need fresh cold whole milk and a cold, clean pitcher. A pitcher with the right spout is essential. Use a straight spout for a one go, continuous pattern and a narrow spout for a drawn pattern. For the best results, place the pitcher in the fridge for 30 minutes before use. This will ensure your milk steams slowly, decreasing the chances of scalding it. Have a liquid thermometer handy so you can check the temperature of your steamed milk.

2 Milk Steaming Process

Make sure the steam wand starts at the bottom of the pitcher. Once the steam is turned on, slowly raise the wand to the top of the milk. For the best results, keep the wand 1cm away from the top of the milk as it rises. You need the milk between 60-65°C with a glossy, full bodied foam and no air bubbles. Once the milk is up to temperature take the steamer out.

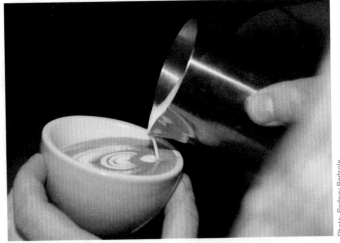

Photo: Rodney Bedsole

3 The Perfect Espresso

For the ideal shot use 7-8 grams of ground espresso. Make sure your espresso is fresh and has a thick, strong layer of crema. Pull the perfect shot between 21-24 seconds. Don't let your espresso sit for more than 10 seconds without adding milk.

4 Pouring Technique

Before you pour make sure there are no air bubbles. If you see any, swirl the milk and pound the pitcher on the counter to get rid of them. Hold the cup slightly tilted and make sure you are comfortable with how you are holding the cup. Whatever pattern you pour, it has to focus on contrast, symmetry and detail.

For all beginners I would recommend the Rosetta pattern, it is the easiest and will give you the best results.

Coffee Cocktails

by **Sam Trevethyen**, Grind

We all love a coffee in the morning and a cocktail in the evening (or the afternoon!). However, in recent years we have seen an explosion of cafés and bars venturing into a cocktail offering environment that blends the two.

Why Coffee & Cocktails?

It's simple, they are the perfect pairing. The rise of specialty coffee perfectly marries the rise of the artisanal approach to bartending. Weird and wonderful spiriting, mixed with a whole cornucopia of different coffees, different brew methods, homemade syrups and who knows what else!

A bit of History

All good drinks need a good story, and this is no exception. Rumour has it that the legendary bartender Dick Bradsell (who sadly passed away last year) gave birth to this title while working at the Soho Brasserie on Greek Street. An unnamed Model (it was the 90's, use your imagination) asked him for a drink that would 'wake her up'. A few shakes later, she got exactly what she wanted.

The Perfect Espresso Martini

This is an easy one. Start with an amazing, freshly pulled espresso shot. Add Vodka and Sugar Syrup. Shake vigorously over ice and double strain into a chilled coupe glass.

One of the reasons we have had so much success at Grind with this drink is a combination of the fact we put every shot of espresso used to order (you need the crema on the shot to be fresh to give you that rich creamy head we all know and love) and we only use coffee, vodka and espresso. After all, it's safe to say coffee and Grind are more than friends.

How did we get into it?

At Grind, we started opening our original site (Shoreditch Grind) rather organically - we were building an awesome vibe during the day, and then shutting the doors and chucking people out at 6pm - why not keep the party going we thought? Not to mention the financial sense behind getting more out

of a space you pay rent on 24/7. For us, as with many, the jump happened with the Espresso Martini. We now have 9 sites across London, but our approach to coffee cocktails has not changed since experimenting in the evenings of Shoreditch Grind. Simple, powerful combinations, blending fresh ingredients that look awesome.

Education & Training

by **Edwin Harrison**, Co-owner, the Artisan Coffee School

The London third wave coffee scene is well established and thriving. So let's look behind the coffee machines for a moment to better understand what impact education and training has on your daily cup of coffee. Making coffee is a complex art and science; any number of small variables, from plantation to barista, can make the difference between a mouthwatering cup and one that ends up being poured down the drain. Owners and managers spend hours focusing on training in order to drive their coffee shops forward and do justice to the coffee growers, roasters and other professionals who have in some way contributed to delivering those amazing beans to our grinder hoppers.

To understand where coffee training and education has arrived today, it's useful to take a brief look at its history. The explosion of branded coffee shop chains in the 1990s lead to the birth of the barista manual, Manuals served to formalise training, systems and techniques by introducing a workflow process for baristas to follow. Together with mass training sessions, the barista manual successfully addressed problems of inconsistency and the coffee chains flourished, but little progress was made to realise coffee's full potential.

The complexity and potential of coffee was too great to be boxed up into a manual or process; the third wave independents were eager to take coffee to the next level. Top baristas started to get excited about what could be achieved through experimentation; everything from milk texturing to coffee flavour profiles came under meticulous scrutiny. Baristas challenged conventional wisdom and investigated the science behind coffee making to understand how it could be improved. Today a new breed of dedicated training schools has emerged exploring coffee theory as well as practical brewing skills. What's more, coffee schools are no longer the preserve of industry professionals, they now offer classes tailored specifically to interested coffee lovers wishing to improve their home brewing.

An introductory barista course run over one or two days would typically include theory with a discussion on processing techniques, different roast types, and establish what flavours we are looking to achieve. The white board will then turn into something you would expect to see in an in-depth physics presentation as coffee enthusiasts discover how to create their own brew ratio. This process alone indicates just how much influence the barista has over the coffee they produce.

Then it's on to the machine, working out variables and learning how to keep these consistent is fundamental to success.

Exploring extraction times, tamping and grind adjustments are just some of the many aspects covered and the trainer will always bring it back to what impact your actions have on the flavour of the coffee. This is key to developing a deeper knowledge of the process you are responsible for. This approach to training becomes infectious as suddenly the world of coffee begins to unfold in front of students' eyes. This is why we see so many students progress from the barista foundation courses through to intermediate and professional level.

The industry as a whole has stepped up and taken notice of this revolution in education. The Speciality Coffee Association of Europe (SCAE) addressed the wide gap in formalised training, gathering top industry figures to formalise a structure with inspiration from the wine industry. The result is the Coffee Diploma System, taking a modular form incorporating the many different aspects of coffee education, and assessed with exams. Many coffee schools, offer SCAE accredited courses in addition to running their own classes.

The rise of coffee schools demonstrates that the industry is taking the next big step and realising that barista training is not a single shadow shift at the start of a job, but an ongoing process that has a very significant impact on the success of a business; from staff retention to the consistency and quality of coffee they serve.

Coffee Glossary

Acidity: the pleasant tartness of a coffee. Examples of acidity descriptors include lively and flat. One of the principal attributes evaluated by professional tasters when determining the quality of a coffee.

AeroPress: a hand-powered coffee brewer marketed by Aerobie Inc., and launched in 2005. Consists of two cylinders, one sliding within the other, somewhat resembling a large syringe. Water is forced through ground coffee held in place by a paper filter, creating a concentrated filter brew.

Affogato: one or more scoops of vanilla ice cream topped with a shot of espresso, served as a dessert.

Americano, Caffè Americano: a long coffee consisting of espresso with hot water added on top. Originates from the style of coffee favoured by American GIs stationed in Europe during WWII.

Arabica, Coffea arabica: the earliest cultivated species of coffee tree and the most widely grown, Arabica accounts for approximately 70% of the world's coffee. Superior in quality to Robusta, it is more delicate and is generally grown at higher altitudes.

Aroma: the fragrance produced by brewed coffee. Examples of aroma descriptors include earthy, spicy and floral. One of the principal attributes evaluated by professional tasters when determining the quality of a coffee.

Barista: a professional person skilled in making coffee, particularly one working at an espresso bar.

Blend: a combination of coffees from different countries or regions. Mixed together, they achieve a balanced flavour profile no single coffee can offer alone.

Body: describes the heaviness, thickness or relative weight of coffee on the tongue. One of the principal attributes evaluated by professional tasters when determining the quality of a coffee.

Bottomless portafilter, naked portafilter: a portafilter without spouts, allowing espresso to flow directly from the bottom of the filter basket into the cup. Allows the extraction to be monitored visually.

Brew group: the assembly protruding from the front of an espresso machine consisting of the grouphead, portafilter and basket. The brew group must be heated to a sufficient temperature to produce a good espresso.

Brew pressure: pressure of 9 bar is required for espresso extraction.

Brew temperature: the water temperature at the point of contact with coffee. Optimum brew temperature varies by extraction method. Espresso brew temperature is typically 90-95°C. A stable brew temperature is crucial for good espresso.

Brew time, extraction time: the contact time between water and coffee. Espresso brew time is typically 25-30 seconds. Brew times are dictated by a variety of factors including the grind coarseness and degree of roast.

Burr set: an integral part of a coffee grinder. Consists of a pair of rotating steel discs between which coffee beans are ground. Burrs are either flat or conical in shape.

Café con leche: a traditional Spanish coffee consisting of espresso topped with scalded milk.

Caffeine: an odourless, slightly bitter

alkaloid responsible for the stimulating effect of coffee.

Cappuccino: a classic Italian coffee comprising espresso, steamed milk and topped with a layer of foam. Traditionally served in a 6oz cup and sometimes topped with powdered chocolate or cinnamon.

Capsule: a self-contained, pre-ground, pre-pressed portion of coffee, individually sealed inside a plastic capsule. Capsule brewing systems are commonly found in domestic coffee machines. Often compatible only with certain equipment brands.

Chemex: A type of pour over coffee brewer with a distinctive hourglass-shaped vessel. Invented in 1941, the Chemex has become regarded as a design classic and is on permanent display at the Museum of Modern Art in New York City.

Cherry: the fruit of the coffee plant. Each cherry contains two coffee seeds (beans).

Cold brew: Cold brew refers to the process of steeping coffee grounds in room temperature or cold water for an extended period. Cold brew coffee is not to be confused with iced coffee.

Cortado: a traditional short Spanish coffee consisting of espresso cut with a small quantity of steamed milk. Similar to an Italian piccolo.

Crema: the dense caramel-coloured layer that forms on the surface of an espresso. Consists of emulsified oils created by the dispersion of gases in liquid at high pressure. The presence of crema is commonly equated with a good espresso.

Cupping: a method by which professional tasters perform sensory evaluation of coffee. Hot water is poured over ground coffee and left to extract. The taster first samples the aroma, then tastes the coffee by slurping it from a spoon.

Decaffeinated: coffee with approximately 97% or more of its naturally occurring caffeine removed is classified as decaffeinated.

Dispersion screen, shower screen: a component of the grouphead that ensures even distribution of brewing water over the coffee bed in the filter basket.

Dosage: the mass of ground coffee used for a given brewing method. Espresso dosage is typically 7-10g of ground coffee (14-20g for a double).

Double espresso, doppio: typically 30-50ml extracted from 14-20g of ground coffee. The majority of coffee venues in this guide serve double shots as standard.

Drip method: a brewing method that allows brew water to seep through a bed of ground coffee by gravity, not pressure.

Espresso: the short, strong shot of coffee that forms the basis for many other coffee beverages. Made by forcing hot water at high pressure through a compressed bed of finely ground coffee.

Espresso machine: in a typical configuration, a pump delivers hot water from a boiler to the brew group, where it is forced under pressure through ground coffee held in the portafilter. A separate boiler delivers steam for milk steaming.

Extraction: the process of infusing coffee with hot water to release flavour, accomplished either by allowing ground coffee to sit in hot water for a period of time or by forcing hot water through ground coffee under pressure.

Coffee Glossary contd.

Filter method: any brewing method in which water filters through a bed of ground coffee. Most commonly used to describe drip method brewers that use a paper filter to separate grounds from brewed coffee.

Flat white: an espresso-based beverage first made popular in Australia and New Zealand. Made with a double shot of espresso with finely steamed milk and a thin layer of microfoam. Typically served as a 5-6oz drink with latte art.

Flavour: the way a coffee tastes. Flavour descriptors include nutty and earthy. One of the principal attributes evaluated by professional tasters when determining the quality of a coffee.

French press, plunger pot, cafetiere: a brewing method that separates grounds from brewed coffee by pressing them to the bottom of the brewing receptacle with a mesh filter attached to a plunger.

Froth, foam: created when milk is heated and aerated, usually with hot steam from an espresso machine's steam wand. Used to create a traditional cappuccino.

Green coffee, green beans: unroasted coffee. The dried seeds from the coffee cherry.

Grind: the degree of coarseness to which coffee beans are ground. A crucial factor in determining the nature of a coffee brew. Grind coarseness should be varied in accordance with the brewing method. Methods involving longer brew times call for a coarse grind. A fine grind is required for brew methods with a short extraction time such as espresso.

Grinder: a vital piece of equipment for making coffee. Coffee beans must be ground evenly for a good extraction. Most commonly motorised, but occasionally manual. Burr grinders are the best choice for an even grind.

Group: see Brew Group

Grouphead: a component of the brew group containing the locking connector for the portafilter and the dispersion screen.

Honey process, pulped natural, semi-washed: a method of processing coffee where the cherry is removed (pulped), but the beans are sun-dried with mucilage intact. Typically results in a sweet flavour profile with a balanced acidity.

Latte, caffè latte: an Italian beverage made with espresso combined with steamed milk, traditionally topped with foamed milk and served in a glass. Typically at least 8oz in volume, usually larger.

Latte art: the pattern or design created by pouring steamed milk on top of espresso. Only finely steamed milk is suitable for creating latte art. Popular patterns include the rosetta and heart.

Lever espresso machine: lever machines use manual force to drive a piston that generates the pressure required for espresso extraction. Common in the first half of the 20th century, but now largely superseded by electric pump-driven machines. Lever machines retain a small but passionate group of proponents.

Long black: a coffee beverage made by adding an espresso on top of hot water. Similar to an Americano, but usually shorter and the crema is preserved.

Macchiato: a coffee beverage consisting of espresso 'stained' with a dash of steamed milk (espresso macchiato) or a tall glass of steamed milk 'stained' with espresso (latte macchiato).

Macrofoam: stiff foam containing large bubbles used to make a traditional cappuccino. Achieved by incorporating a greater quantity of air during the milk steaming process.

Matcha: Finely ground powder of specially grown and processed green tea. The matcha plants are shade-grown for three weeks before harvest.

Microfoam: the preferred texture of finely-steamed milk for espresso-based coffee drinks. Essential for pouring latte art. Achieved by incorporating a lesser quantity of air during the milk steaming process.

Micro-lot coffee: coffee originating from a small, discrete area within a farm, typically benefiting from conditions favourable to the development of a particular set of characteristics. Micro-lot coffees tend to fetch higher prices due to their unique nature.

Mocha, caffè mocha: similar to a caffè latte, but with added chocolate syrup or powder.

Natural process: a simple method of processing coffee where whole cherries (with the bean inside) are dried on raised beds under the sun. Typically results in a lower acidity coffee with a heavier body and exotic flavours.

Over extracted: describes coffee with a bitter or burnt taste, resulting from ground coffee exposed to hot water for too long.

Peaberry: a small, round coffee bean formed when only one seed, rather than the usual two, develops in a coffee cherry. Peaberry beans produce a different flavour profile,

typically lighter-bodied with higher acidy.

Piccolo: a short Italian coffee beverage made with espresso topped with an equal quantity of steamed milk. Traditionally served in a glass.

Pod: a self-contained, pre-ground, pre-pressed puck of coffee, individually wrapped inside a perforated paper filter. Mostly found in domestic espresso machines. Often compatible only with certain equipment brands.

Pour over: a type of drip filter method in which a thin, steady stream of water is poured slowly over a bed of ground coffee contained within a filter cone.

Pouring kettle: a kettle with a narrow swan-neck spout specifically designed to deliver a steady, thin stream of water.

Portafilter: consists of a handle (usually plastic) attached to a metal cradle that holds the filter basket. Inserted into the group head and locked in place in preparation for making an espresso. Usually features a single or double spout on the underside to direct the flow of coffee into a cup.

Portafilter basket: a flat bottomed, bowl-shaped metal insert that sits in the portafilter and holds a bed of ground coffee. The basket has an array of tiny holes in the base allowing extracted coffee to seep through and pour into a cup.

Puck: immediately after an espresso extraction, the bed of spent coffee grounds forms compressed waste matter resembling a small hockey puck.

Pull: the act of pouring an espresso. The term originates from the first half of the 20th century when manual machines were the norm, and baristas pulled a lever to

Coffee Glossary contd.

create an espresso.

Ristretto: a shorter 'restricted' shot of espresso. Made using the same dose and brew time as for a regular espresso, but with less water. The result is a richer and more intense beverage.

Roast: the process by which green coffee is heated in order to produce coffee beans ready for consumption. Caramelisation occurs as intense heat converts starches in the bean to simple sugars, imbuing the bean with flavour and transforming its colour to a golden brown.

Robusta, Coffea canephora: the second most widely cultivated coffee species after arabica, robusta accounts for approximately 30% of the world's coffee. Robusta is hardier and grown at lower altitudes than arabica. It has a much higher caffeine content than arabica, and a less refined flavour. Commonly used in instant coffee blends.

Shot: a single unit of brewed espresso.

Single origin, single estate: coffee from one particular region or farm.

Siphon brewer, vacuum brewer: an unusual brewing method that relies on the action of a vacuum to draw hot water through coffee from one glass chamber to another. The resulting brew is remarkably clean.

Small batch: refers to roasting beans in small quantities, typically between 4-24kg, but sometimes larger.

Speciality coffee: a premium quality coffee scoring 80 points or above (from a total of 100) in the SCAA grading scale.

Steam wand: the protruding pipe found on an espresso machine that supplies hot steam used to froth and steam milk.

Stovetop, moka pot: a brewing method that makes strong coffee (but not espresso). Placed directly on a heat source, hot water is forced by steam pressure from the lower chamber to the upper chamber, passing through a bed of coffee.

Tamp: the process of distributing and pressing ground coffee into a compact bed within the portafilter basket in preparation for brewing espresso. The degree of pressure applied during tamping is a key variable in espresso extraction. Too light and the brew water will percolate rapidly (tending to under extract), too firm and the water flow will be impeded (tending to over extract).

Tamper: the small pestle-like tool used to distribute and compact ground coffee in the filter basket.

Third wave coffee: the movement that treats coffee as an artisanal foodstuff rather than a commodity product. Quality coffee reflects its terroir, in a similar manner to wine.

Under extracted: describes coffee that has not been exposed to brew water for long enough. The resulting brew is often sour and thin-bodied.

V60: a popular type of pour over coffee brewer marketed by Hario. The product takes its name from the 60° angle of the V-shaped cone. Typically used to brew one or two cups only.

Washed process: one of the most common methods of processing coffee cherries. Involves fermentation in tanks of water to remove mucilage. Typically results in a clean and bright flavour profile with higher acidity.

Whole bean: coffee that has been roasted but not ground.

A-Z List of Coffee Venues

A-Z List of Coffee Venues contd.

* NEW
◊ TOP 35

A-Z List of Coffee Venues contd.